P&P COMPANY

Don't Trust Every Thought

Rethink Your Thoughts

ER. PARWINDER KUMAR
9/15/2023

Table of Contents

<u>Introduction: The Unreliable Narrator in Your Head</u>

The mind is a powerful storyteller. From the moment we wake up to the moment we fall asleep, our thoughts weave an intricate narrative that shapes our perception of the world and ourselves. This inner monologue, composed of a continuous stream of thoughts, judgments, and interpretations, guides our actions and reactions. But what if this narrator isn't always reliable? What if the stories we tell ourselves are riddled with distortions, biases, and falsehoods? This is the premise of "Don't Trust Every Thought," a journey into the intricate landscape of the mind and an exploration of the unreliable narrator that resides within each of us.

Our thoughts are influenced by a multitude of factors, including our upbringing, cultural background, personal experiences, and emotional state. They are not always objective truths but rather subjective interpretations. These interpretations can be skewed by cognitive biases—systematic patterns of deviation from norm or rationality in judgment. For example, confirmation bias leads us to favor information that confirms our preexisting beliefs, while ignoring evidence that contradicts them. Similarly, negativity bias makes us pay more attention to negative experiences than positive ones, which can distort our overall outlook on life.

One classic example of an unreliable thought is the phenomenon known as "catastrophizing." This occurs when we anticipate the worst possible outcome of a situation, often with little or no evidence to support such a dire prediction. For instance, if you're waiting for feedback on a project at work, you might start to worry that your boss hated it and is considering firing you, even though there's no indication that this is the case. Such thoughts can create unnecessary stress and anxiety, influencing our behavior and decisions in unproductive ways.

The stories we tell ourselves can also be heavily influenced by past experiences. Trauma, for instance, can leave a lasting imprint on the mind, leading to persistent negative thoughts and beliefs. Someone who has experienced betrayal may struggle with trust issues, interpreting innocent actions by others as potential threats. These thoughts are not a reflection of the current reality but rather echoes of past pain. Recognizing this can be a powerful step toward healing and breaking free from the grip of these unreliable thoughts.

Social and cultural conditioning further complicate our inner narrative. From a young age, we are bombarded with messages about who we should be, how we should act, and what we should value. These messages come from family, friends, media, and society at large. Over time, they become internalized and shape our self-concept and worldview. However, these externally imposed beliefs may not align with our true selves. For instance, societal standards of beauty can lead individuals to develop a distorted self-image, believing they are unattractive or inadequate despite evidence to the contrary.

The mind's tendency to wander and ruminate can also contribute to the unreliability of our thoughts. Rumination involves repetitive thinking about a particular issue, often focusing on its negative aspects. This can create a vicious cycle of negative thinking that is hard to break. For example, after making a mistake, instead of acknowledging it and moving on, you might obsess over it, repeatedly telling yourself how stupid you were. This not only reinforces a negative self-view but also prevents you from learning from the experience and moving forward.

Given these tendencies, it becomes crucial to develop a more discerning approach to our thoughts. One effective strategy is mindfulness, which involves paying attention to the present moment without judgment. By observing our thoughts as they arise, we can begin to notice patterns and question their validity. This practice can create a space between our thoughts and our reactions, allowing us to respond more thoughtfully rather than react impulsively.

Another powerful tool is cognitive restructuring, a technique used in cognitive-behavioral therapy (CBT). This involves identifying and challenging distorted thoughts and replacing them with more balanced and rational ones. For instance, if you catch yourself thinking, "I'll never succeed," you can counter this by reminding yourself of past successes and the efforts you're putting in to achieve your goals. Over time, this practice can help rewire your thinking patterns, making your inner narrator more reliable and supportive.

It's also important to cultivate self-compassion. Often, we are our own harshest critics, holding ourselves to impossibly high standards and berating ourselves for perceived failures. Practicing self-compassion involves treating yourself with the same kindness and understanding that you would offer a friend in a similar situation. This can soften the impact of negative thoughts and create a more nurturing internal environment.

In conclusion, our thoughts are powerful but not infallible. The narrator in our head can lead us astray with distortions, biases, and untruths. By recognizing this, we can begin to question and challenge our thoughts, developing a more accurate and supportive inner narrative. "Don't Trust Every Thought" invites you to embark on this journey of self-discovery and mental clarity, providing tools and insights to navigate the complex landscape of your mind and transform the way you relate to your thoughts.

...

<u>Chapter 1: The Origins of Our Thoughts</u>

Our thoughts are the building blocks of our perception, the lens through which we interpret the world around us. They shape our emotions, influence our behaviors, and ultimately, define our reality. But where do these thoughts come from? Understanding the origins of our thoughts is essential to understanding their nature, reliability, and impact on our lives. This chapter delves into the complex interplay of factors that give rise to our thoughts, including biological mechanisms, psychological processes, and sociocultural influences.

The Biological Basis of Thought

The genesis of thought begins in the brain, the intricate organ that orchestrates our mental processes. Neurons, the fundamental units of the brain and nervous system, communicate with each other through electrical impulses and chemical signals. This neural communication forms the basis of our thoughts, memories, and perceptions.

Neuroscientists have identified specific brain regions involved in different aspects of thought. For example, the prefrontal cortex, located at the front of the brain, is crucial for higher-order functions such as planning, decision-making, and social behavior. The hippocampus, nestled deep within the brain, plays a key role in forming and retrieving memories. These regions, among others, interact in complex ways to produce the rich tapestry of our thoughts.

Neurotransmitters, the brain's chemical messengers, also play a significant role in shaping our thoughts. For instance, serotonin is involved in regulating mood and anxiety, while dopamine influences reward and motivation. Imbalances in these chemicals can lead to various mental health conditions, affecting the nature and quality of our thoughts. For example, low levels of serotonin are associated with depression, which can manifest as persistent negative thinking.

The Psychological Roots of Thought

While the biological framework provides the hardware for thought, psychological processes are the software that drives it. Cognitive psychology, the study of mental processes, offers insights into how we think, perceive, remember, and learn.

One key concept in cognitive psychology is the idea of schemas—mental structures that help us organize and interpret information. Schemas are built from our experiences and knowledge and serve as cognitive shortcuts, allowing us to quickly make sense of new information. For example, when you think of a "dog," your schema for dogs might include characteristics like four legs, fur, and barking. These schemas help us navigate the world efficiently but can also lead to biases and stereotypes if they become too rigid or are based on limited experiences.

Another important aspect of thought formation is the role of automatic thoughts. These are spontaneous, involuntary thoughts that arise in response to specific situations. They are often shaped by our underlying beliefs and attitudes. For example, if you hold a belief that you are not good enough, you might have automatic thoughts like "I always mess up" when faced with a challenging task. These thoughts can influence our emotions and behaviors, often without us being fully aware of their impact.

Cognitive distortions are another psychological phenomenon that can shape our thoughts. These are systematic errors in thinking that can lead to negative emotions and maladaptive behaviors. Common cognitive distortions include black-and-white thinking (seeing things in extremes, with no middle ground), overgeneralization (drawing broad conclusions from a single event), and personalization (believing that external events are directly related to oneself). Recognizing and challenging these distortions is a key component of cognitive-behavioral therapy (CBT), a widely used therapeutic approach.

The Influence of Early Experiences

Our early experiences, particularly in childhood, have a profound impact on the formation of our thoughts and beliefs. Attachment theory, developed by psychologist John Bowlby, emphasizes the importance of early relationships in shaping our mental and emotional development. According to this theory, the quality of the bond between a child and their primary caregiver influences their sense of security and their ability to form healthy relationships later in life.

Secure attachment, characterized by consistent and responsive caregiving, leads to positive self-concepts and a belief in the reliability of others. Conversely, insecure attachment, resulting from inconsistent or neglectful caregiving, can lead to negative self-concepts and mistrust in others. These early patterns of attachment are internalized and can shape our thoughts and behaviors throughout our lives.

Traumatic experiences in childhood, such as abuse or neglect, can also have lasting effects on our thought processes. Trauma can disrupt the normal development of the brain and lead to heightened sensitivity to stress and negative emotions. This can result in persistent negative thoughts, hypervigilance, and difficulty regulating emotions. Understanding the impact of early experiences on our thought patterns can be a crucial step in healing and personal growth.

The Role of Social and Cultural Influences

Our thoughts are not formed in isolation; they are deeply influenced by the social and cultural context in which we live. From the moment we are born, we are immersed in a web of social relationships and cultural norms that shape our beliefs, values, and behaviors.

Social learning theory, developed by psychologist Albert Bandura, emphasizes the role of observation and imitation in learning. According to this theory, we acquire new behaviors and thoughts by observing others, particularly those we consider role models. For example, children often mimic the behavior and attitudes of their parents, peers, and teachers. This process of social learning continues throughout our lives, influencing our thoughts and actions.

Cultural norms and values also play a significant role in shaping our thoughts. Culture encompasses the shared beliefs, practices, and customs of a group of people, and it provides a framework for understanding the world. For example, individualistic cultures, which emphasize personal autonomy and self-expression, may encourage thoughts related to personal achievement and independence. In contrast, collectivistic cultures, which prioritize group harmony and interdependence, may foster thoughts related to social responsibility and connectedness.

Media, including television, film, and social media, is another powerful cultural influence on our thoughts. The content we consume can shape our perceptions of reality, influence our attitudes, and affect our mental health. For instance, exposure to unrealistic standards of beauty in the media can contribute to body image issues and negative self-thoughts. Similarly, social media platforms, with their curated portrayals of people's lives, can lead to feelings of inadequacy and comparison.

The Interplay of Emotion and Thought

Emotions and thoughts are inextricably linked, each influencing the other in a dynamic interplay. Our emotional state can shape the content and tone of our thoughts, while our thoughts can amplify or diminish our emotions.

Emotional experiences often serve as triggers for specific thoughts. For example, feeling anxious might lead to thoughts about potential threats or dangers, while feeling happy might lead to more optimistic and positive thoughts. This bidirectional relationship between emotion and thought is central to our overall mental well-being.

The concept of emotional regulation refers to the processes by which we influence our emotions, how they are experienced, and how they are expressed. Effective emotional regulation involves being aware of our emotions, understanding the thoughts that accompany them, and employing strategies to manage them constructively. Mindfulness and cognitive-behavioral techniques are effective tools for improving emotional regulation and fostering a healthier thought-life.

The Importance of Metacognition

Metacognition, or "thinking about thinking," is the awareness and understanding of one's own thought processes. It involves recognizing the nature of our thoughts, evaluating their accuracy and usefulness, and making conscious choices about how to respond to them.

Developing metacognitive skills can help us become more aware of the automatic and often unconscious thoughts that influence our emotions and behaviors. By bringing these thoughts into conscious awareness, we can begin to question and challenge them, fostering a more balanced and accurate internal narrative.

One practical way to cultivate metacognition is through reflective practices such as journaling or meditation. These practices provide a space to observe and reflect on our thoughts, gaining insights into patterns and underlying beliefs. Over time, this can lead to greater self-awareness and more intentional, mindful thinking.

Conclusion: The Path to Thoughtful Awareness

Understanding the origins of our thoughts is a multifaceted journey that encompasses biological, psychological, social, and cultural dimensions. By exploring these influences, we can gain deeper insights into the nature of our thoughts and their impact on our lives.

Recognizing that our thoughts are shaped by a complex interplay of factors can empower us to question their validity and challenge unhelpful patterns. Developing awareness and metacognitive skills can help us become more discerning and intentional in our thinking, leading to greater mental clarity and emotional well-being.

"Don't Trust Every Thought" invites you to continue this journey of exploration and self-discovery. By examining the origins of your thoughts and cultivating a mindful and reflective approach, you can transform your relationship with your inner narrative, fostering a more balanced and supportive mindset.

...

<u>Chapter 2: Cognitive Biases and Distortions</u>

Human cognition, despite its remarkable capabilities, is far from perfect. Our minds are susceptible to a variety of biases and distortions—systematic patterns of deviation from rationality in judgment and decision-making. These cognitive biases and distortions shape our perceptions, influence our decisions, and often lead us astray. In this chapter, we will explore some of the most common cognitive biases and distortions, understand their origins, and learn how to mitigate their effects.

Understanding Cognitive Biases

Cognitive biases are inherent in the human brain's information processing system. They arise from the mental shortcuts, or heuristics, that our brains use to simplify complex decision-making processes. While these shortcuts are generally helpful and efficient, they can also lead to errors in judgment.

1. **Confirmation Bias**

Confirmation bias is the tendency to search for, interpret, and remember information in a way that confirms our preexisting beliefs. This bias affects our ability to objectively evaluate evidence and can reinforce faulty thinking. For example, if you believe that a particular political candidate is corrupt, you are more likely to notice and remember news stories that support this belief while disregarding evidence to the contrary. Confirmation bias can lead to polarized thinking and prevent us from considering alternative perspectives.

2. **Anchoring Bias**

Anchoring bias occurs when we rely too heavily on the first piece of information we receive (the "anchor") when making decisions.

Subsequent judgments are influenced by this initial information, even if it is irrelevant or misleading. For example, if you see a shirt priced at $100 and later find it on sale for $50, the initial price of $100 serves as an anchor, making the sale price seem like a great deal, even if $50 might still be overpriced for that item.

3. Availability Heuristic

The availability heuristic is a mental shortcut that relies on immediate examples that come to mind. When evaluating the likelihood of an event, we tend to overestimate its probability based on how easily we can recall instances of it. For example, after hearing about several airplane accidents in the news, you might overestimate the danger of flying, even though statistically, air travel is safer than driving. This heuristic can lead to skewed perceptions of risk and probability.

4. Hindsight Bias

Hindsight bias, also known as the "I-knew-it-all-along" effect, is the tendency to see events as having been predictable after they have already occurred. This bias can lead to overconfidence in our ability to predict outcomes and can distort our understanding of past events. For example, after a sports team wins a game, you might believe that the outcome was obvious all along, even if you were unsure before the game started. Hindsight bias can impair our ability to learn from past experiences and make accurate future predictions.

5. Overconfidence Bias

Overconfidence bias is the tendency to overestimate our own abilities, knowledge, and the accuracy of our predictions. This bias can lead to poor decision-making and risk-taking. For example, a stock trader might believe they have exceptional insight into market movements, leading them to make risky investments. Overconfidence can prevent us from seeking feedback and considering alternative viewpoints.

Exploring Cognitive Distortions

Cognitive distortions are irrational and exaggerated thought patterns that can perpetuate negative emotions and mental health issues. These distortions often arise from deep-seated beliefs and can significantly impact our mental well-being.

1. **All-or-Nothing Thinking**

All-or-nothing thinking, also known as black-and-white thinking, involves seeing things in extremes, with no middle ground. For example, you might think, "If I don't get an A on this test, I'm a complete failure." This type of thinking can create unrealistic expectations and lead to feelings of inadequacy and disappointment. Recognizing that most situations exist in shades of gray, rather than black and white, can help mitigate this distortion.

2. **Overgeneralization**

Overgeneralization involves drawing broad, sweeping conclusions based on a single event or limited evidence. For example, if you fail one job interview, you might conclude, "I'll never get a job." This distortion can lead to a negative self-concept and hopelessness. Challenging overgeneralizations by examining the evidence and considering alternative explanations can help reduce their impact.

3. **Mental Filtering**

Mental filtering involves focusing exclusively on negative aspects of a situation while ignoring positive ones. For example, after receiving feedback on a presentation, you might fixate on one critical comment and disregard all the positive feedback. This distortion can contribute to a negative outlook and low self-esteem. Practicing balanced thinking by acknowledging both positive and negative aspects of a situation can help counteract mental filtering.

4. Discounting the Positive

Discounting the positive involves dismissing positive experiences or achievements as insignificant or unimportant. For example, you might attribute a success to luck rather than your own abilities. This distortion can prevent you from fully appreciating your strengths and accomplishments. Recognizing and celebrating your successes, no matter how small, can help combat this distortion.

5. Jumping to Conclusions

Jumping to conclusions involves making assumptions without sufficient evidence. This distortion can take two forms: mind reading and fortune telling. Mind reading involves assuming you know what others are thinking, while fortune telling involves predicting negative outcomes. For example, you might think, "My boss is going to hate my proposal" without any concrete evidence. Challenging these assumptions by seeking evidence and considering alternative scenarios can help reduce this distortion.

6. Catastrophizing

Catastrophizing involves expecting the worst possible outcome in any situation. For example, if you make a small mistake at work, you might fear that you'll be fired. This distortion can create excessive anxiety and prevent you from taking reasonable risks. Practicing realistic thinking by evaluating the likelihood and impact of worst-case scenarios can help mitigate catastrophizing.

7. **Emotional Reasoning**

Emotional reasoning involves interpreting situations based on your emotions rather than objective evidence. For example, if you feel anxious, you might conclude that something bad is going to happen. This distortion can create a self-fulfilling prophecy, where negative emotions lead to negative outcomes. Recognizing that emotions are not always accurate reflections of reality and seeking evidence to support your conclusions can help reduce emotional reasoning.

8. **Should Statements**

Should statements involve imposing rigid expectations on yourself or others, often leading to feelings of guilt, frustration, or resentment. For example, you might think, "I should always be perfect" or "People should always treat me fairly." These unrealistic expectations can create a sense of failure and dissatisfaction. Replacing should statements with more flexible and realistic expectations can help reduce their impact.

9. **Labeling and Mislabeling**

Labeling involves assigning negative labels to yourself or others based on isolated incidents. For example, if you make a mistake, you might label yourself as "stupid" or "a failure." Mislabeling involves using emotionally loaded language to describe a situation. For example, you might describe a minor setback as a "disaster." These distortions can reinforce negative self-concepts and increase emotional distress. Challenging labels by focusing on specific behaviors rather than global judgments can help mitigate their effects.

10. **Personalization**

Personalization involves taking responsibility for events outside your control or blaming yourself for negative outcomes. For example, if a friend is upset, you might assume it's because of something you did, even if there is no evidence to support this. Personalization can create feelings of guilt and inadequacy. Recognizing the limits of your responsibility and considering alternative explanations can help reduce personalization.

Mitigating Cognitive Biases and Distortions

While cognitive biases and distortions are a natural part of human thinking, there are strategies to mitigate their effects and promote more rational and balanced thinking.

1. Awareness and Self-Reflection

The first step in addressing cognitive biases and distortions is to become aware of them. Regular self-reflection and mindfulness practices can help you notice when these patterns arise. Keeping a thought journal, where you record and analyze your thoughts, can also be a useful tool for identifying and challenging biases and distortions.

2. Challenging Assumptions

Actively questioning and challenging your assumptions can help reduce the impact of cognitive biases and distortions. When you notice a biased or distorted thought, ask yourself questions like, "What evidence do I have for this thought?" "Are there alternative explanations?" and "Am I considering all relevant information?"

3. Seeking Feedback

Seeking feedback from others can provide a different perspective and help counteract your own biases. Discussing your thoughts and decisions with trusted friends, family members, or colleagues can offer new insights and challenge your assumptions.

4. Balanced Thinking

Practicing balanced thinking involves considering both positive and negative aspects of a situation. When you notice a negative thought, make an effort to identify at least one positive aspect as well. This can help create a more nuanced and realistic perspective.

5. Mindfulness and Cognitive-Behavioral Techniques

Mindfulness practices, such as meditation and mindful breathing, can help you become more aware of your thoughts and create a space between stimulus and response. Cognitive-behavioral techniques, such as cognitive restructuring, involve identifying and challenging distorted thoughts and replacing them with more balanced and rational ones. These techniques can help reframe your thinking and reduce the impact of biases and distortions.

6. Developing Emotional Regulation Skills

Improving your ability to regulate your emotions can help reduce the influence of emotional reasoning and other distortions. Techniques such as deep breathing, progressive muscle relaxation, and visualization can help manage intense emotions and create a calmer state of mind.

7. Embracing Uncertainty

Accepting that uncertainty is a natural part of life can help reduce the need for black-and-white thinking and catastrophizing. Recognizing that not everything can be predicted or controlled can create a more flexible and adaptive mindset.

Conclusion: Towards Clearer Thinking

Understanding and addressing cognitive biases and distortions is essential for cultivating clearer, more rational thinking. Throughout this chapter, we've explored various biases and distortions that affect how we perceive, interpret, and respond to the world around us. These biases arise from evolutionary adaptations and psychological mechanisms that once served survival purposes but can lead to errors in judgment in modern-day contexts.

By recognizing these biases and distortions, we can begin to mitigate their effects and develop more balanced and accurate thought processes. Awareness is the first step—being mindful of our thought patterns and noticing when biases or distortions arise. This awareness allows us to pause, reflect, and challenge our automatic thoughts, replacing them with more reasoned and evidence-based thinking.

Practicing self-reflection and keeping a thought journal can help us identify recurring biases and distortions in our thinking. By documenting our thoughts and analyzing them over time, we can gain insights into the underlying beliefs and assumptions that drive our behaviors and decisions.

Seeking feedback from others is another valuable strategy for mitigating biases. Trusted friends, family members, or colleagues can offer different perspectives and challenge our assumptions, helping us see situations more objectively.

Mindfulness techniques, such as meditation and mindful breathing, can enhance our awareness of thoughts as they arise and help us respond more intentionally rather than reactively. These practices create a space between stimulus and response, allowing us to choose how we interpret and act upon information.

Cognitive-behavioral techniques, including cognitive restructuring, are effective tools for challenging and modifying distorted thinking patterns. By identifying cognitive distortions such as overgeneralization or catastrophizing, and replacing them with more balanced and realistic thoughts, we can reduce negative emotional responses and improve decision-making.

Emotional regulation skills are also crucial in managing the impact of biases and distortions. Techniques such as deep breathing, progressive muscle relaxation, and visualization can help regulate intense emotions that may amplify cognitive distortions like emotional reasoning or personalization.

Finally, embracing uncertainty and acknowledging the limitations of our knowledge can foster a more open-minded and adaptive approach to thinking. Recognizing that we cannot control every outcome and that life is inherently uncertain allows us to tolerate ambiguity and approach challenges with resilience and flexibility.

In conclusion, while cognitive biases and distortions are natural aspects of human cognition, we have the ability to mitigate their impact through awareness, reflection, and intentional practice. By cultivating clearer thinking, we can enhance our decision-making abilities, improve our relationships, and promote overall well-being. The journey towards clearer thinking is ongoing, but by taking proactive steps to understand and address biases and distortions, we empower ourselves to navigate life's complexities with greater wisdom and insight.

...

Chapter 3: The Power of Perspective

Perspective is the lens through which we view the world. It encompasses our beliefs, values, experiences, and attitudes, shaping how we interpret events, interact with others, and make sense of our lives. In this chapter, we will explore the profound influence of perspective on our thoughts, emotions, and behaviors, and examine how cultivating awareness of different perspectives can enhance empathy, resilience, and personal growth.

Understanding Perspective

Perspective is not just a passive observation; it actively constructs our reality. It determines what we pay attention to, how we interpret information, and the meanings we assign to events. Our perspective is shaped by a multitude of factors, including:

1. **Personal Experiences:** Our unique life experiences, from childhood through adulthood, influence our perspective. Positive experiences may lead to an optimistic outlook, while negative experiences can foster pessimism or distrust.

2. **Cultural Background:** Cultural norms, values, and traditions play a significant role in shaping our perspective. They define what is considered acceptable, desirable, or taboo within a particular society or community.

3. **Beliefs and Values:** Our beliefs about ourselves, others, and the world around us shape our perspective. These beliefs can be influenced by religion, philosophy, personal ethics, and moral principles.

4. **Social Context:** Interactions with family, friends, peers, and colleagues contribute to our perspective. Social relationships provide opportunities for learning, growth, and the exchange of ideas.

5. **Emotional State:** Our current emotional state can influence our perspective, affecting how we interpret events and make decisions. For example, feelings of anger or fear may color our perceptions and lead to biased judgments.

The Influence of Perspective on Thought Patterns

Perspective profoundly impacts our thought patterns and cognitive processes. It can shape:

1. **Interpretation of Events**: The same event can be interpreted differently based on one's perspective. For example, a setback at work may be viewed as an opportunity for growth by one person and as a personal failure by another.

2. **Problem-Solving Approaches:** Different perspectives offer alternative ways of approaching problems and challenges. A diverse team, for instance, benefits from varied viewpoints that contribute to innovative solutions.

3. **Decision-Making:** Our perspective influences the criteria we use to make decisions and the outcomes we anticipate. A business leader considering an expansion may weigh financial risks differently depending on their perspective on growth and stability.

4. **Emotional Regulation:** Perspective can affect how we regulate our emotions. By reframing situations from different angles, we can shift our emotional responses and enhance resilience.

The Role of Empathy in Shifting Perspectives

Empathy—the ability to understand and share the feelings of another—plays a crucial role in expanding our perspective. When we empathize with others, we step into their shoes and see the world through their eyes. This process fosters:

1. **Connection and Understanding:** Empathy builds bridges of understanding between individuals and promotes compassionate interactions. It helps us recognize common humanity despite differences in perspective.

2. **Conflict Resolution:** In conflicts, empathizing with opposing viewpoints can lead to collaborative problem-solving and compromise. It allows us to acknowledge the validity of different perspectives while seeking common ground.

3. **Personal Growth:** Empathy encourages personal growth by challenging our assumptions and broadening our worldview. It prompts us to question our own biases and consider alternative interpretations.

Developing Awareness of Different Perspectives

Developing awareness of different perspectives involves:

1. **Active Listening:** Paying attention to others' viewpoints without judgment or interruption promotes understanding and empathy. It allows us to grasp the nuances of diverse experiences and perspectives.

2. **Seeking Diversity:** Engaging with individuals from diverse backgrounds—whether cultural, socioeconomic, or ideological—

exposes us to a range of perspectives. This exposure stimulates critical thinking and expands our worldview.

3. **Reflective Practice:** Reflecting on our own perspective and how it influences our thoughts and actions fosters self-awareness. Journaling or meditation can facilitate introspection and insight into our biases.

4. **Challenging Assumptions:** Actively questioning our assumptions and considering alternative perspectives encourages cognitive flexibility. This practice enables us to adapt to changing circumstances and navigate complexity with greater clarity.

Overcoming Cognitive Biases through Perspective-Taking

Perspective-taking is a cognitive process that involves mentally stepping into another person's shoes and viewing a situation from their perspective. It can help counteract cognitive biases such as:

1. **Confirmation Bias:** By seeking out information that challenges rather than confirms our beliefs, we can broaden our perspective and reduce bias.

2. **Anchoring Bias:** Considering alternative anchors or viewpoints can mitigate the influence of initial impressions or information.

3. **Availability Heuristic:** Actively seeking diverse perspectives and information sources can mitigate the availability heuristic by exposing us to a broader range of experiences and opinions.

4. **Hindsight Bias:** Engaging in perspective-taking can prevent us from falling into the trap of hindsight bias by acknowledging the complexity and unpredictability of events.

Leveraging Perspective for Personal Growth and Well-Being

Perspective is not only a lens through which we view the world but also a tool for personal growth and well-being:

1. **Enhanced Resilience:** By cultivating awareness of different perspectives, we develop resilience in the face of adversity. Viewing challenges from multiple angles allows us to adapt and find creative solutions.

2. **Improved Relationships:** Understanding and respecting diverse perspectives strengthens interpersonal relationships. It fosters empathy, communication, and mutual respect, laying the foundation for meaningful connections.

3. **Expanded Creativity:** Exposure to diverse perspectives fuels creativity and innovation. By integrating diverse ideas and viewpoints, we generate novel solutions and approaches.

4. **Reduced Stress:** Adopting a broader perspective can alleviate stress by reducing the intensity of emotional reactions to challenges. It encourages a more balanced and adaptive response to difficulties.

Conclusion: Embracing the Diversity of Perspectives

In conclusion, perspective is a dynamic and influential force that shapes our thoughts, emotions, and behaviors. By understanding the factors that contribute to our perspective—such as personal experiences, cultural background, beliefs, and social interactions—we gain insight into how we perceive and navigate the world.

Developing awareness of different perspectives and cultivating empathy are essential practices for expanding our worldview and fostering personal growth. These practices enable us to challenge our own biases, enhance our decision-making abilities, and build meaningful connections with others.

As you continue your journey of self-discovery and exploration of perspective, reflect on how embracing diversity of thought can enrich your life and contribute to a more compassionate and inclusive society. By valuing and respecting diverse perspectives, we can collectively create a world where empathy, understanding, and mutual respect thrive.

...

<u>Chapter 4: Emotion vs. Logic</u>

The interplay between emotion and logic is a fundamental aspect of human cognition and decision-making. Emotions and logic represent two distinct but interconnected systems that influence how we perceive, process information, and make choices in our daily lives. In this chapter, we will explore the roles of emotion and logic, their impact on decision-making processes, and strategies for achieving a balanced approach to navigating their complexities.

The Nature of Emotion

Emotions are complex psychological and physiological responses to internal and external stimuli. They encompass a wide range of feelings, from joy and love to anger and fear, each serving distinct functions in our lives:

1. **Function of Emotions:**
   - **Adaptive Responses:** Emotions evolved as adaptive responses to help us navigate and respond to our environment effectively. For example, fear triggers a fight-or-flight response in the face of danger, preparing the body to react quickly.
   - **Communication:** Emotions serve as a form of social communication, conveying information about our internal states and intentions to others. Facial expressions, gestures, and vocal intonations convey emotional cues that facilitate social interactions and relationships.
   - **Motivation:** Emotions play a crucial role in motivating behavior. For instance, desire and anticipation motivate us to pursue goals and rewards, while aversion and disappointment steer us away from threats and negative outcomes.

2. **Components of Emotion:**

- **Physiological:** Emotions are accompanied by physiological changes, such as increased heart rate, hormonal fluctuations, and changes in facial expressions and body posture.

- **Cognitive:** Emotions involve cognitive appraisal processes, where we evaluate the significance of stimuli and events based on our personal goals, values, and past experiences.

- **Subjective Experience:** Emotions are also characterized by subjective feelings, such as happiness, sadness, or anxiety, which color our subjective experience of the world.

The Role of Emotion in Decision-Making

Emotions exert a powerful influence on decision-making processes, often interacting with and sometimes overriding logical considerations:

1. **Intuitive Decision-Making:** Emotions play a central role in intuitive decision-making processes, where decisions are made quickly based on gut feelings, past experiences, and emotional cues. Intuition can be valuable in situations where immediate action is required or when faced with complex, ambiguous information.

2. **Risk Assessment:** Emotions influence how we perceive and assess risk. For example, fear may lead to risk aversion, while excitement or overconfidence may increase risk-taking behavior. These emotional responses can impact financial decisions, career choices, and health-related behaviors.

3. **Moral Reasoning:** Emotions contribute to moral reasoning and ethical decision-making. Compassion, guilt, and empathy guide our judgments about right and wrong, influencing behaviors such as helping others, honesty, and adherence to ethical principles.

4. **Affect Heuristic:** The affect heuristic is a mental shortcut where decisions are influenced by emotions associated with past experiences or preconceived notions. For example, positive emotions towards a brand may influence purchasing decisions, regardless of logical arguments about product features.

The Role of Logic and Reasoning

Logic and reasoning, on the other hand, represent deliberate, systematic processes of evaluating information, drawing conclusions, and making decisions based on evidence and principles of rationality:

1. **Analytical Thinking:** Logical reasoning involves breaking down complex problems into component parts, analyzing evidence, and applying deductive or inductive reasoning to reach conclusions. Analytical thinking is essential in fields such as science, mathematics, and critical analysis.

2. **Critical Thinking:** Critical thinking entails evaluating arguments and evidence, identifying logical fallacies, and assessing the validity and reliability of information. It helps us make informed decisions and avoid cognitive biases that distort rational judgment.

3. **Planning and Problem-Solving:** Logical reasoning plays a crucial role in planning and problem-solving processes. It allows us to weigh alternative courses of action, anticipate consequences, and develop strategies to achieve goals effectively.

4. **Decision Analysis:** Decision analysis frameworks, such as cost-benefit analysis or decision trees, use logical reasoning to evaluate options, quantify risks, and optimize decision outcomes based on objective criteria.

The Conflict Between Emotion and Logic

Despite their complementary roles, emotion and logic can sometimes conflict, leading to challenges in decision-making:

1. **Emotional Bias:** Emotional biases, such as confirmation bias or availability heuristic, can distort logical reasoning and lead to irrational decision-making. For example, clinging to a losing investment due to emotional attachment rather than objective financial analysis.

2. **Impulsivity vs. Prudence:** Emotions can lead to impulsive decisions that prioritize short-term gratification over long-term benefits. Conversely, excessive reliance on logic may overlook emotional considerations and human values essential for well-being and fulfillment.

3. **Complex Situations:** In complex situations with conflicting information or uncertain outcomes, emotional responses and logical analysis may yield divergent recommendations. Balancing these perspectives requires careful consideration of both emotional and logical factors.

Strategies for Balancing Emotion and Logic

Achieving a balanced approach to decision-making involves integrating emotional awareness with logical reasoning. Strategies include:

1. **Emotional Awareness:** Cultivating mindfulness and emotional intelligence enhances awareness of emotional states and their influence on decision-making. Techniques such as meditation, journaling, or therapy promote self-reflection and emotional regulation.

2. **Pause and Reflect:** Before making important decisions, take time to pause and reflect on your emotional responses and logical considerations. Consider how emotions may be influencing your judgment and whether additional information or perspectives are needed.

3. **Seek Diverse Perspectives:** Engage in dialogue with others to gain diverse perspectives and feedback on decisions. Collaborative decision-making fosters empathy, expands understanding, and mitigates the influence of personal biases.

4. **Utilize Decision-Making Frameworks:** Incorporate decision-making frameworks that combine logical analysis with emotional considerations. For example, decision matrices or pros and cons lists can structure evaluations while acknowledging emotional preferences and values.

5. **Balance Information Processing:** Balance information processing by integrating intuitive, emotional responses with systematic, analytical reasoning. Trust your instincts while verifying assumptions and testing hypotheses through logical inquiry.

6. **Long-Term Perspective:** Consider the long-term implications of decisions on personal goals, values, and well-being. Balance short-term emotional impulses with strategic planning and foresight to achieve desired outcomes over time.

Integrating Emotion and Logic for Optimal Decision-Making

Integrating emotion and logic enables us to make informed, adaptive decisions that align with our values and goals:

1. **Synergistic Decision-Making:** Embrace the synergy between emotion and logic to leverage their respective strengths. Emotional

insights can inspire creativity and passion, while logical reasoning provides structure and clarity.

2. **Adaptive Flexibility:** Cultivate adaptive flexibility in decision-making by adjusting strategies based on changing circumstances and new information. Embrace uncertainty and complexity as opportunities for growth and learning.

3. **Personal Growth:** Embrace challenges as opportunities for personal growth and self-discovery. Reflect on past decisions to identify lessons learned and apply insights to future decision-making processes.

4. **Resilience and Well-Being:** Foster resilience and well-being by nurturing a balanced approach to decision-making. Embrace emotions as valuable sources of information while employing logical analysis to mitigate biases and achieve optimal outcomes.

Conclusion: Embracing the Dual Forces of Emotion and Logic

In conclusion, the dynamic interplay between emotion and logic shapes our perceptions, influences decision-making processes, and defines our experiences as human beings. By understanding the roles of emotion and logic—acknowledging their strengths and limitations—we can cultivate a balanced approach to decision-making that enhances personal fulfillment, resilience, and well-being.

As you navigate the complexities of life, consider how integrating emotional awareness with logical reasoning can empower you to make thoughtful, informed decisions. Embrace the richness of emotional experiences while harnessing the power of logical analysis to achieve clarity, purpose, and fulfillment in your journey. By embracing the dual forces of emotion and logic, you pave the way for growth, resilience, and meaningful connections in all aspects of your life.

...

Chapter 5: The Role of Past Experiences

Our past experiences serve as a profound influence on our present thoughts, emotions, behaviors, and decision-making processes. Throughout our lives, we accumulate a wealth of experiences—both positive and negative—that shape our perceptions of ourselves, others, and the world around us. In this chapter, we will explore the multifaceted role of past experiences, how they contribute to our identity and beliefs, influence our present actions, and provide opportunities for growth and transformation.

Formation of Personal Identity

Our past experiences play a crucial role in shaping our sense of identity—the core beliefs, values, and self-perceptions that define who we are. Key factors influencing identity formation include:

1. **Early Childhood Experiences:** Early childhood experiences, such as interactions with caregivers, family dynamics, and early socialization, lay the foundation for our sense of self. Positive experiences, such as secure attachments and nurturing environments, contribute to healthy self-esteem and resilience. Conversely, adverse experiences, such as trauma or neglect, can impact self-concept and emotional well-being.

2. **Educational and Social Experiences:** Educational experiences, peer relationships, and social interactions during adolescence and young adulthood further shape identity development. Academic achievements, friendships, and social roles influence self-confidence, aspirations, and attitudes towards success and failure.

3. **Cultural and Societal Influences:** Cultural norms, values, and societal expectations also shape identity formation. Cultural heritage,

religious beliefs, and societal roles contribute to our understanding of self and influence behaviors, decisions, and relationships.

4. **Life Transitions and Milestones:** Life transitions, such as career changes, parenthood, or retirement, provide opportunities for reflection and growth. These milestones influence identity by prompting shifts in priorities, values, and self-perceptions.

Influence on Beliefs and Perspectives

Past experiences contribute to the formation of beliefs, attitudes, and perspectives that shape how we interpret and respond to the world:

1. **Core Beliefs:** Core beliefs are fundamental assumptions about ourselves, others, and the world, often formed through repeated experiences and reinforced over time. Positive experiences may foster beliefs in resilience, self-efficacy, and trust, while negative experiences can lead to beliefs of inadequacy, distrust, or pessimism.

2. **Cognitive Schemas:** Cognitive schemas are mental frameworks that organize and interpret information. They develop through experiences and influence perception, memory, and decision-making. For example, a person with a schema of "trustworthiness" may interpret ambiguous social cues positively, whereas someone with a schema of "distrust" may perceive the same cues negatively.

3. **Expectations and Assumptions:** Past experiences shape expectations about future events and interactions. Positive experiences may foster optimistic expectations and openness to new opportunities, while negative experiences can lead to caution, skepticism, or avoidance.

Impact on Emotional Responses

Past experiences profoundly influence emotional responses to current events and interactions:

1. **Emotional Memory**: Emotional memories associated with past experiences influence emotional responses in similar situations. Positive memories may evoke feelings of happiness, security, or comfort, while negative memories can trigger anxiety, sadness, or anger.

2. **Emotional Regulation:** The ability to regulate emotions is influenced by past experiences and learned coping strategies. Effective emotional regulation promotes resilience and adaptive responses to stress, adversity, and uncertainty.

3. **Trauma and Emotional Healing:** Traumatic experiences can have lasting effects on emotional well-being and require specialized interventions for healing and recovery. Supportive relationships, therapy, and self-care practices can facilitate emotional healing and resilience.

Influence on Decision-Making and Behavior

Past experiences inform decision-making processes and behavioral patterns:

1. **Decision-Making Strategies:** Decision-making strategies are influenced by past experiences, learned outcomes, and perceived risks and rewards. Positive experiences of success may encourage risk-taking and initiative, while experiences of failure may lead to caution and deliberation.

2. **Behavioral Patterns:** Behavioral patterns, such as habits, coping mechanisms, and interpersonal skills, develop through repeated experiences and reinforcement. Adaptive behaviors promote personal growth and well-being, while maladaptive behaviors may require intervention and change.

3. **Learning and Adaptation:** Learning from past experiences enables adaptation to changing circumstances and challenges. Reflection on past decisions and outcomes fosters insight, resilience, and informed decision-making in future situations.

Opportunities for Growth and Transformation

Past experiences provide opportunities for growth, learning, and personal transformation:

1. **Reflection and Insight:** Reflecting on past experiences promotes self-awareness, insight, and understanding of personal strengths and areas for development. Journaling, therapy, and mindfulness practices facilitate introspection and growth.

2. **Resilience and Adaptability:** Resilience—the ability to bounce back from adversity—is cultivated through overcoming challenges and learning from setbacks. Adapting to new environments, roles, and relationships fosters resilience and strengthens coping skills.

3. **Behavioral Change:** Awareness of past behaviors and their consequences facilitates behavioral change and personal development. Setting goals, seeking support, and practicing new skills promote sustainable behavior change and well-being.

Integrating Past Experiences for Personal Empowerment

Integrating past experiences involves acknowledging their influence while actively shaping present and future outcomes:

1. **Acceptance and Forgiveness:** Acceptance of past experiences, including mistakes and challenges, promotes self-compassion and emotional healing. Forgiveness—of oneself and others—fosters resilience and frees energy for personal growth.

2. **Learning and Adaptation:** Learning from past experiences involves extracting lessons, identifying strengths, and applying insights to current situations. Adaptive responses promote flexibility, creativity, and proactive problem-solving.

3. **Goal Setting and Visioning:** Setting goals aligned with personal values and aspirations empowers individuals to pursue meaningful outcomes. Visioning—imagining future possibilities—motivates action and fosters optimism and purpose.

Conclusion: Embracing the Journey of Self-Discovery

In conclusion, past experiences serve as a dynamic and evolving influence on our identities, beliefs, emotions, behaviors, and decision-making processes. By understanding the multifaceted role of past experiences—acknowledging their impact, learning from challenges, and embracing opportunities for growth—we empower ourselves to navigate life's complexities with resilience, purpose, and authenticity.

As you continue your journey of self-discovery and personal development, reflect on the ways in which past experiences have shaped your values, beliefs, and aspirations. Embrace the power of reflection, learning, and adaptation to cultivate resilience, compassion, and personal fulfillment. By integrating past experiences into your present journey, you pave the way for continued growth, transformation, and meaningful contributions to your own life and the world around you.

...

Chapter 6: Identifying and Challenging False Beliefs

Beliefs shape our perceptions, guide our decisions, and influence our behaviors. They are the lenses through which we interpret the world and ourselves. While many beliefs are based on valid information and experiences, others may be distorted or inaccurate. In this chapter, we will explore the nature of beliefs, strategies for identifying false beliefs, and effective methods for challenging and reshaping them to promote personal growth and well-being.

Understanding Beliefs

Beliefs are mental representations of reality that influence our thoughts, emotions, and behaviors. They are formed through a variety of factors, including:

1. **Experiences:** Direct experiences, both positive and negative, contribute to the formation of beliefs. For example, a positive experience of receiving praise may lead to beliefs about competence, while a negative experience of rejection may lead to beliefs about unworthiness.

2. **Socialization:** Beliefs are shaped by cultural norms, societal values, family upbringing, and peer influences. These social contexts provide frameworks for understanding the world and defining personal identity.

3. **Cognitive Processes:** Cognitive processes such as perception, memory, and reasoning contribute to the development and maintenance of beliefs. Confirmation bias, for instance, reinforces existing beliefs by selectively attending to information that confirms them.

4. **Emotional Influences:** Emotions play a significant role in belief formation and reinforcement. Emotional experiences associated with beliefs can strengthen their impact on thoughts and behaviors.

Types of Beliefs

Beliefs can be categorized into various types based on their content and function:

1. **Core Beliefs:** Core beliefs are fundamental assumptions about oneself, others, and the world. They often develop early in life and shape one's identity and worldview. Examples include beliefs about competence, worthiness, and trust.

2. **Intermediate Beliefs:** Intermediate beliefs are beliefs that stem from core beliefs and influence specific thoughts and behaviors. They are more flexible and context-dependent than core beliefs but still contribute to overall cognitive schemas.

3. **Automatic Thoughts:** Automatic thoughts are fleeting, spontaneous thoughts that arise in response to situations or triggers. They are influenced by core and intermediate beliefs and can impact mood and behavior in the moment.

4. **Cultural and Societal Beliefs:** Cultural and societal beliefs reflect shared values, norms, and ideologies within a community or society. They influence collective attitudes, behaviors, and social structures.

Identifying False Beliefs

False beliefs are beliefs that are distorted, irrational, or not supported by evidence. Identifying false beliefs involves critical reflection and examination of their origins, validity, and impact. Key indicators of false beliefs include:

1. **Evidence Contradiction:** False beliefs often lack empirical evidence or contradict factual information. They may be based on anecdotal experiences, misconceptions, or cognitive biases.

2. **Overgeneralization:** Overgeneralization occurs when one draws broad conclusions based on limited or isolated experiences. Beliefs that generalize from single incidents or specific contexts may be inaccurate or exaggerated.

3. **Cognitive Biases:** Cognitive biases, such as confirmation bias, availability heuristic, or emotional reasoning, can distort perceptions and reinforce false beliefs. Recognizing these biases is crucial for evaluating the validity of beliefs.

4. **Emotional Intensity:** False beliefs may be associated with intense emotional reactions, such as fear, anger, or shame. Emotional intensity can cloud judgment and reinforce irrational beliefs.

Strategies for Challenging False Beliefs

Challenging false beliefs involves a systematic approach to examining their validity, exploring alternative perspectives, and fostering cognitive flexibility. Effective strategies include:

1. **Reality Testing:** Reality testing involves gathering objective evidence and examining the facts that support or contradict a belief. Question assumptions and seek diverse sources of information to verify or challenge the validity of the belief.

2. **Cognitive Restructuring:** Cognitive restructuring is a cognitive-behavioral technique that involves identifying and replacing irrational or distorted thoughts with more balanced and realistic alternatives. Steps include:

- **Identifying Automatic Thoughts:** Recognize automatic thoughts that accompany emotional reactions or specific situations.

- **Evaluating Evidence:** Assess the evidence supporting or refuting the automatic thought. Consider alternative explanations or interpretations.

- **Generating Alternative Thoughts:** Develop alternative, balanced thoughts that reflect a more accurate assessment of the situation.

- **Testing the New Thought:** Test the new thought by observing its impact on emotions and behaviors. Practice integrating the new perspective into daily life.

3. **Behavioral Experiments:** Behavioral experiments involve testing beliefs through behavioral actions or experiments. Engage in activities that challenge the belief or provide opportunities for new learning and experiences. Observe the outcomes and reassess the belief based on empirical evidence.

4. **Mindfulness and Metacognition:** Mindfulness practices promote awareness of thoughts, emotions, and beliefs without judgment. Metacognition—the ability to reflect on and monitor one's thinking—facilitates critical self-awareness and insight into belief patterns.

5. **Seeking Perspective:** Seek feedback and perspectives from others to gain alternative viewpoints and challenge cognitive biases. Engage in open dialogue, listen actively, and consider diverse perspectives to broaden understanding and promote cognitive flexibility.

Overcoming Common Challenges

Challenging false beliefs may encounter resistance or obstacles. Common challenges include:

1. **Emotional Resistance:** Emotional attachment to beliefs, even false ones, can create resistance to change. Validate emotions while exploring underlying beliefs and their origins.

2. **Fear of Uncertainty**: Beliefs provide a sense of certainty and security. Fear of uncertainty or ambiguity may deter individuals from questioning or revising beliefs.

3. **Cognitive Rigidity:** Rigidity in thinking patterns can inhibit flexibility and adaptation. Practice cognitive flexibility through exposure to new information, alternative perspectives, and diverse experiences.

4. **Perseverance:** Challenging false beliefs requires persistence and commitment to personal growth. Set realistic goals, monitor progress, and celebrate achievements to sustain motivation.

Integrating New Beliefs for Personal Growth

Integrating new, more adaptive beliefs promotes personal growth, resilience, and well-being:

1. **Self-Compassion:** Cultivate self-compassion and acceptance throughout the process of challenging and revising beliefs. Recognize that beliefs are malleable and evolve with new experiences and insights.

2. **Authenticity:** Align beliefs with personal values, aspirations, and goals to foster authenticity and purpose. Embrace beliefs that support personal growth, resilience, and positive relationships.

3. **Continuous Learning:** Embrace a growth mindset that values continuous learning and adaptation. View challenges as opportunities for self-discovery, growth, and expanding perspectives.

4. **Supportive Relationships**: Surround yourself with supportive relationships that encourage open dialogue, empathy, and mutual respect. Share insights, challenges, and successes in challenging false beliefs.

Conclusion: Empowering Personal Transformation

In conclusion, identifying and challenging false beliefs is a transformative journey that empowers individuals to cultivate self-awareness, resilience, and authenticity. By understanding the origins and impact of beliefs, adopting effective strategies for evaluation and restructuring, and fostering cognitive flexibility and emotional resilience, individuals can navigate life's challenges with clarity, purpose, and adaptive responses.

As you embark on your own journey of self-discovery and belief exploration, reflect on the beliefs that shape your thoughts, emotions, and behaviors. Embrace the process of challenging false beliefs with curiosity, compassion, and a commitment to personal growth. By integrating new, more adaptive beliefs, you create opportunities for empowerment, fulfillment, and meaningful contributions to your own life and the world around you.

...

Chapter 7: The Influence of Social and Cultural Conditioning

Social and cultural conditioning encompasses the powerful impact of societal norms, cultural values, and social influences on individual beliefs, behaviors, and identities. From childhood through adulthood, individuals are immersed in environments shaped by family, peers, media, education, and broader societal institutions. In this chapter, we will explore how social and cultural conditioning shapes perceptions, influences decision-making processes, and contributes to the construction of personal and collective identities.

Understanding Social and Cultural Conditioning

Social and cultural conditioning refers to the process through which individuals internalize and conform to societal norms, values, beliefs, and behaviors. This conditioning occurs through various mechanisms:

1. **Family Dynamics:** Families serve as primary agents of socialization, transmitting cultural values, norms, and traditions across generations. Parental guidance, caregiving practices, and familial roles shape early social and emotional development.

2. **Peer Influences:** Peers play a significant role in socialization, particularly during adolescence and young adulthood. Peer groups establish norms of behavior, social expectations, and peer acceptance criteria that influence individual attitudes and behaviors.

3. **Education and Institutions:** Educational institutions, religious organizations, and community groups reinforce cultural values, impart knowledge, and promote social conformity. Curriculum, teachings, and institutional practices shape cognitive development and social identity formation.

4. **Media and Technology:** Mass media, digital platforms, and popular culture disseminate cultural narratives, social ideals, and stereotypes. Media representations influence perceptions of gender roles, societal norms, and cultural identities.

Impact on Beliefs and Values

Social and cultural conditioning shapes individual beliefs, values, and worldviews through various mechanisms:

1. **Normative Influence:** Norms are unwritten rules and expectations that guide behavior within a society or group. Conformity to social norms reinforces acceptance and belonging, while deviance may lead to social sanctions or ostracism.

2. **Cultural Values:** Cultural values represent collective preferences, priorities, and moral principles within a society. Values such as individualism, collectivism, egalitarianism, or hierarchy influence decision-making, interpersonal relationships, and societal structures.

3. **Implicit Bias:** Implicit biases are unconscious attitudes and stereotypes that affect perceptions, decisions, and behaviors. These biases are shaped by cultural conditioning and social experiences, impacting interactions with diverse individuals and groups.

Formation of Social Identity

Social identity refers to the part of an individual's self-concept derived from perceived membership in social groups. Social identity is influenced by:

1. **Group Affiliation:** Identification with social groups, such as family, ethnicity, religion, nationality, or socioeconomic status, shapes social

identity and collective belonging. Group memberships contribute to shared values, beliefs, and cultural practices.

2. **Intersectionality**: Intersectionality considers how multiple social identities (e.g., race, gender, class) intersect to influence experiences of privilege, discrimination, and social status. Intersectional perspectives highlight the complexity of identity formation and social inequalities.

3. **Identity Development:** Identity development involves exploring and integrating personal and social identities over the lifespan. Individuals navigate identity crises, achieve identity commitments, and adapt to changing social contexts and roles.

Influence on Decision-Making Processes

Social and cultural conditioning influences decision-making processes through:

1. **Social Norms and Expectations:** Compliance with social norms guides decisions about behavior, appearance, and interpersonal interactions. Conformity to social expectations promotes social cohesion but may limit individual autonomy and creativity.

2. **Role Expectations:** Roles define expected behaviors, responsibilities, and obligations within social contexts (e.g., parent, student, employee). Fulfilling role expectations requires aligning personal beliefs and behaviors with societal norms and professional standards.

3. **Peer Pressure and Influence:** Peer pressure exerts influence on decision-making through social approval, conformity, and the desire for acceptance. Peer group dynamics impact choices related to relationships, leisure activities, and risk-taking behaviors.

Cultural Perspectives on Well-Being and Fulfillment

Cultural perspectives shape perceptions of well-being, happiness, and fulfillment:

1. **Cultural Models of Happiness:** Cultural norms and values influence definitions of happiness, success, and life satisfaction. Individualistic cultures prioritize personal achievement and autonomy, while collectivist cultures emphasize family harmony and social relationships.

2. **Spirituality and Meaning:** Cultural and religious beliefs provide frameworks for understanding existential questions and seeking meaning in life. Spiritual practices, rituals, and community involvement promote psychological well-being and resilience.

3. **Social Support and Community:** Cultural contexts influence social support networks, community cohesion, and caregiving practices. Strong social ties and community engagement enhance emotional support, coping resources, and overall quality of life.

Challenging Social and Cultural Conditioning

Challenging social and cultural conditioning involves critical reflection, cultural awareness, and conscious efforts to promote diversity, equity, and inclusion:

1. **Critical Consciousness:** Critical consciousness involves questioning dominant narratives, power structures, and systemic inequalities. Recognize and challenge social injustices, biases, and discriminatory practices within cultural contexts.

2. **Cultural Competence:** Cultivate cultural competence by understanding and respecting diverse cultural perspectives, practices, and communication styles. Embrace diversity, advocate for equity, and promote inclusive environments in personal and professional settings.

3. **Self-Reflection and Awareness:** Reflect on personal biases, stereotypes, and assumptions shaped by social and cultural conditioning. Engage in introspection, dialogue, and continuous learning to expand perspectives and challenge implicit biases.

Nurturing Cultural Sensitivity and Inclusivity

Nurturing cultural sensitivity and inclusivity fosters respectful engagement with diverse individuals and communities:

1. **Empathy and Perspective-Taking:** Practice empathy and perspective-taking to understand others' experiences, values, and cultural backgrounds. Listen actively, validate diverse perspectives, and cultivate mutual respect in interpersonal interactions.

2. **Cross-Cultural Communication:** Develop effective cross-cultural communication skills to navigate cultural differences and promote meaningful dialogue. Adapt communication styles, clarify misunderstandings, and foster collaborative relationships.

3. **Advocacy and Social Change:** Advocate for social justice, equity, and human rights within cultural contexts. Support initiatives that promote cultural diversity, empower marginalized groups, and challenge discriminatory practices.

Conclusion: Embracing Cultural Awareness and Diversity

In conclusion, social and cultural conditioning profoundly shapes individual beliefs, behaviors, identities, and societal norms. By understanding the influences of socialization, cultural values, and group dynamics, individuals can navigate diverse cultural contexts with empathy, respect, and cultural competence. Embrace cultural awareness, challenge biases, and foster inclusive environments to promote social justice, equity, and collective well-being.

As you reflect on the impact of social and cultural conditioning in your own life, consider how cultural values, societal norms, and group affiliations shape your beliefs, behaviors, and interactions with others. Embrace diversity, celebrate cultural richness, and contribute to creating inclusive communities that honor and respect diverse perspectives and identities. Through collective efforts, we can cultivate a more just, equitable, and harmonious society that values cultural diversity and promotes human flourishing for all.

...

Chapter 8: Mindfulness and Metacognition

Mindfulness and metacognition are powerful cognitive processes that enhance self-awareness, promote cognitive flexibility, and facilitate personal growth. In this chapter, we explore the principles of mindfulness and metacognition, their applications in daily life, and their transformative effects on mental well-being and decision-making.

Understanding Mindfulness

Mindfulness is the practice of intentionally focusing attention on the present moment without judgment. Rooted in ancient contemplative traditions, mindfulness has gained recognition in modern psychology and neuroscience for its therapeutic benefits and cognitive enhancements. Key aspects of mindfulness include:

1. **Present-Moment Awareness:** Mindfulness involves directing attention to the present moment experiences, including sensations, thoughts, emotions, and external stimuli. By cultivating present-moment awareness, individuals enhance clarity, concentration, and responsiveness.

2. **Non-Judgmental Acceptance:** Mindfulness encourages observing experiences without evaluative judgment or criticism. Accepting thoughts and emotions with openness and compassion fosters emotional resilience, reduces reactivity, and promotes psychological well-being.

3. **Intentional Attention:** Mindfulness involves purposefully directing attention to chosen focal points, such as breath sensations, bodily sensations, or sensory perceptions. Training attentional control strengthens cognitive processes and reduces distractibility.

Benefits of Mindfulness Practice

Mindfulness practice offers numerous benefits for mental, emotional, and physical well-being:

1. **Stress Reduction:** Mindfulness techniques, such as deep breathing and body scan exercises, mitigate physiological stress responses and promote relaxation. Regular practice enhances resilience to stressors and improves coping mechanisms.

2. **Emotional Regulation:** Mindfulness cultivates awareness of emotional states and enhances emotional regulation skills. Recognizing and accepting emotions without reactive judgment fosters self-control, empathy, and interpersonal relationships.

3. **Cognitive Clarity:** Mindfulness sharpens cognitive abilities, including attentional focus, working memory, and decision-making. Increased cognitive clarity supports effective problem-solving, creative thinking, and adaptive learning.

4. **Psychological Resilience:** Mindfulness practice builds psychological resilience by fostering adaptive responses to adversity, uncertainty, and life challenges. Developing resilience promotes mental toughness, perseverance, and optimism.

Applications of Mindfulness in Daily Life

Integrating mindfulness into daily routines enhances overall well-being and quality of life:

1. **Mindful Awareness:** Practice mindful awareness during routine activities, such as eating, walking, or commuting. Notice sensory experiences, thoughts, and emotions without distraction or automatic reactions.

2. **Stress Management:** Use mindfulness techniques, such as mindful breathing or progressive muscle relaxation, to alleviate stress and promote relaxation. Create mindful pauses during hectic moments to regain composure and clarity.

3. **Mindful Communication:** Practice active listening and mindful communication in interpersonal interactions. Validate others' perspectives, respond thoughtfully, and cultivate empathy and understanding.

4. **Workplace Effectiveness:** Apply mindfulness techniques to enhance productivity, creativity, and resilience in professional settings. Practice mindful work breaks, prioritize tasks mindfully, and manage workplace stressors effectively.

Metacognition: Thinking About Thinking

Metacognition refers to the ability to monitor, reflect on, and regulate one's cognitive processes. It involves awareness of one's thoughts, problem-solving strategies, learning preferences, and decision-making tendencies. Key components of metacognition include:

1. **Self-Reflection:** Engage in self-reflection to evaluate and analyze thinking processes, beliefs, and assumptions. Identify cognitive strengths, areas for improvement, and learning goals.

2. **Strategic Planning:** Plan and organize cognitive tasks, such as studying, problem-solving, or decision-making. Use metacognitive strategies, such as setting goals, monitoring progress, and adjusting strategies based on feedback.

3. **Monitoring and Evaluation:** Monitor cognitive performance during tasks to assess comprehension, accuracy, and efficiency.

Reflect on task outcomes, identify errors or misconceptions, and revise strategies for improved performance.

Benefits of Metacognitive Awareness

Metacognitive awareness enhances learning, problem-solving, and decision-making effectiveness:

1. **Enhanced Learning:** Metacognitive strategies, such as summarizing, questioning, and self-explanation, improve comprehension, retention, and application of knowledge. Reflective learning promotes deeper understanding and critical thinking skills.

2. **Improved Problem-Solving:** Apply metacognitive strategies, such as brainstorming, planning, and evaluating alternatives, to solve complex problems effectively. Flexibility in thinking and adaptive problem-solving lead to innovative solutions.

3. **Decision-Making Competence:** Use metacognitive reflection to assess decision-making processes, evaluate options, and anticipate consequences. Enhance decision-making competence by considering multiple perspectives and weighing trade-offs.

Integrating Mindfulness and Metacognition

Integrating mindfulness and metacognition enhances self-awareness, cognitive flexibility, and adaptive functioning:

1. **Awareness of Thought Patterns:** Use mindfulness to observe thought patterns, emotions, and cognitive biases without judgment. Cultivate metacognitive awareness to analyze thinking processes and identify cognitive distortions.

2. **Self-Regulation:** Apply mindfulness techniques, such as mindful breathing or body scan, to regulate emotional responses and promote cognitive control. Use metacognitive strategies to monitor and adjust cognitive strategies for optimal performance.

3. **Reflective Practice:** Combine mindfulness and metacognition in reflective practices, such as journaling, meditation, or guided self-inquiry. Explore personal experiences, insights, and growth opportunities with curiosity and openness.

Cultivating Mindful Metacognition for Personal Growth

Develop mindful metacognition to foster holistic well-being and personal growth:

1. **Holistic Wellness:** Embrace a holistic approach to well-being that integrates physical health, emotional resilience, and cognitive vitality. Practice mindfulness and metacognition to cultivate balance, clarity, and inner harmony.

2. **Continuous Learning:** Adopt a growth mindset that values lifelong learning, self-improvement, and intellectual curiosity. Embrace challenges, seek diverse perspectives, and engage in ongoing self-reflection and growth.

3. **Community and Connection:** Foster supportive relationships and community connections that promote mutual respect, empathy, and collective well-being. Share mindfulness and metacognitive practices to inspire personal and social transformation.

Conclusion: Embracing Mindfulness and Metacognition

In conclusion, mindfulness and metacognition are transformative practices that enhance self-awareness, promote cognitive flexibility, and facilitate personal growth. By cultivating present-moment awareness, non-judgmental acceptance, and metacognitive reflection, individuals develop resilience, creativity, and effective decision-making skills. Embrace mindfulness and metacognition as integral tools for navigating life's challenges with clarity, compassion, and purpose.

As you explore the principles and applications of mindfulness and metacognition in your own life, reflect on their potential to enhance well-being, foster personal growth, and promote positive change. Embrace mindfulness as a pathway to inner peace and metacognition as a tool for cognitive empowerment. Together, these practices empower individuals to cultivate mindful awareness, foster metacognitive reflection, and embrace transformative possibilities for themselves and their communities.

...

<u>Chapter 9: Techniques for Cognitive Restructuring</u>

Cognitive restructuring is a therapeutic approach rooted in cognitive-behavioral therapy (CBT) that aims to identify and challenge irrational or distorted thoughts. By replacing negative or dysfunctional thought patterns with more balanced and realistic ones, cognitive restructuring enhances emotional resilience, promotes adaptive behaviors, and facilitates personal growth. In this chapter, we explore various techniques and strategies for effectively implementing cognitive restructuring in everyday life.

Understanding Cognitive Restructuring

Cognitive restructuring involves recognizing and modifying cognitive distortions or unhelpful thinking patterns that contribute to emotional distress, maladaptive behaviors, and negative beliefs about oneself, others, or the world. Key principles of cognitive restructuring include:

1. **Identifying Automatic Thoughts:** Automatic thoughts are rapid, reflexive thoughts that arise in response to situations or triggers. These thoughts often reflect underlying beliefs or assumptions and influence emotional reactions and behaviors.

2. **Examining Cognitive Distortions:** Cognitive distortions are biased or exaggerated ways of thinking that contribute to negative interpretations and emotional reactions. Common cognitive distortions include all-or-nothing thinking, overgeneralization, catastrophizing, and personalization.

3. **Challenging and Restructuring Thoughts:** Cognitive restructuring involves questioning the accuracy and validity of automatic thoughts and replacing them with more balanced,

evidence-based alternatives. By challenging cognitive distortions, individuals cultivate cognitive flexibility and emotional resilience.

Techniques for Cognitive Restructuring

Effective cognitive restructuring techniques empower individuals to challenge irrational thoughts, modify unhelpful beliefs, and promote psychological well-being. Explore the following techniques to implement cognitive restructuring in practice:

1. **Identifying Thought Patterns:**

   - **Thought Records:** Keep a thought record or journal to track automatic thoughts, emotional reactions, and situational triggers. Record specific situations, associated thoughts, emotions, and behavioral responses.

   - **Mindful Observation:** Practice mindfulness to observe thoughts and emotions without judgment. Notice cognitive patterns, recurring themes, and triggers that contribute to distress or negative beliefs.

2. **Evaluating Evidence:**

   - **Reality Testing:** Engage in reality testing by examining objective evidence that supports or contradicts automatic thoughts. Evaluate the accuracy and reliability of assumptions, predictions, or interpretations.

   - **Socratic Questioning:** Use Socratic questioning techniques to explore the validity and logic of automatic thoughts. Ask probing questions, such as "What evidence supports this thought?" or "What alternative explanations are there?"

3. **Generating Alternative Thoughts:**

- **Alternative Explanations:** Identify alternative explanations or interpretations of the situation. Consider multiple perspectives, possible outcomes, and realistic appraisals that challenge cognitive distortions.

- **Balanced Thinking:** Cultivate balanced thinking by acknowledging strengths and weaknesses, considering potential solutions or coping strategies, and reframing negative situations in a more constructive light.

4. Behavioral Experiments:

- **Testing Assumptions:** Conduct behavioral experiments to test assumptions or beliefs. Engage in new behaviors or activities that challenge fear-based or avoidance behaviors and promote adaptive responses.

- **Outcome Evaluation:** Evaluate the outcomes of behavioral experiments objectively. Notice changes in emotions, behaviors, and perceptions to gain insights into the accuracy of beliefs and the effectiveness of alternative strategies.

5. Graded Exposure:

- **Systematic Desensitization:** Use systematic desensitization techniques to gradually expose oneself to feared or anxiety-provoking situations. Start with mild exposures and progressively increase exposure intensity to reduce anxiety and build confidence.

- **Relaxation Techniques:** Practice relaxation techniques, such as deep breathing, progressive muscle relaxation, or guided imagery, during exposure exercises to manage anxiety symptoms and promote relaxation.

6. Cognitive Distancing:

- **Thought Defusion:** Practice thought defusion techniques to create psychological distance from negative thoughts or intrusive beliefs. View thoughts as passing mental events rather than accurate reflections of reality.

- **Metaphorical Reframing:** Use metaphorical reframing to reframe negative thoughts or self-criticisms in a playful or exaggerated manner. Replace harsh self-talk with humorous or compassionate reinterpretations.

7. Mindfulness-Based Cognitive Therapy (MBCT):

- **Mindfulness Meditation:** Integrate mindfulness meditation practices to enhance awareness of thoughts, emotions, and bodily sensations. Cultivate non-judgmental acceptance and present-moment awareness to reduce reactivity and enhance emotional regulation.

- **Body Scan:** Practice body scan meditation to systematically observe bodily sensations and release tension or discomfort associated with stress or anxiety. Enhance mindfulness of physical and emotional experiences.

Integrating Cognitive Restructuring into Daily Life

Integrating cognitive restructuring techniques into daily routines promotes ongoing personal growth and emotional resilience:

1. **Daily Reflection:** Allocate time for daily reflection to review and challenge automatic thoughts, cognitive distortions, and unhelpful beliefs. Identify triggers, emotional reactions, and opportunities for cognitive restructuring.

2. **Behavioral Activation:** Engage in pleasurable or rewarding activities that promote positive emotions, accomplishment, and social connection. Behavioral activation counters avoidance behaviors and reinforces adaptive coping strategies.

3. **Self-Care Practices:** Prioritize self-care practices, such as adequate sleep, nutritious diet, regular exercise, and relaxation techniques. Physical well-being supports cognitive functioning and emotional stability necessary for effective cognitive restructuring.

4. **Social Support:** Seek social support from trusted friends, family members, or mental health professionals. Discuss thoughts and emotions openly, receive feedback, and gain perspective on challenging situations or beliefs.

Overcoming Challenges in Cognitive Restructuring

Challenges in cognitive restructuring may arise due to emotional resistance, cognitive rigidity, or entrenched beliefs:

1. **Emotional Resistance:** Acknowledge and validate emotional responses associated with challenging thoughts or beliefs. Practice self-compassion, patience, and persistence in navigating discomfort and emotional vulnerability.

2. **Cognitive Rigidity:** Foster cognitive flexibility through exposure to new perspectives, diverse viewpoints, and alternative interpretations. Challenge black-and-white thinking and embrace complexity in understanding oneself and others.

3. **Perseverance:** Maintain motivation and commitment to cognitive restructuring despite setbacks or initial discomfort. Set realistic goals, celebrate progress, and seek support from others to sustain momentum and resilience.

Cultivating Lasting Change and Growth

Cognitive restructuring fosters lasting change and personal growth by promoting adaptive beliefs, enhancing emotional resilience, and empowering proactive behaviors:

1. **Adaptive Beliefs:** Replace negative or distorted beliefs with adaptive, realistic beliefs that support self-confidence, resilience, and positive self-image. Embrace cognitive flexibility and openness to new learning and experiences.

2. **Emotional Resilience:** Develop emotional resilience by cultivating mindfulness, managing stress effectively, and practicing self-regulation skills. Respond to challenges with clarity, composure, and adaptive coping strategies.

3. **Proactive Behaviors:** Engage in proactive behaviors that align with personal values, goals, and aspirations. Take deliberate actions to pursue meaningful activities, foster relationships, and contribute to personal well-being and community involvement.

Conclusion: Empowering Cognitive Restructuring

In conclusion, cognitive restructuring empowers individuals to challenge and replace negative or distorted thoughts with more balanced, realistic interpretations. By applying cognitive restructuring techniques, individuals enhance emotional resilience, promote adaptive behaviors, and foster personal growth. Embrace cognitive flexibility, self-awareness, and proactive change to navigate life's challenges with clarity, confidence, and resilience.

As you explore techniques for cognitive restructuring in your own life, reflect on the impact of automatic thoughts, cognitive distortions, and beliefs on your emotions, behaviors, and decision-making. Embrace cognitive restructuring as a transformative process that promotes psychological well-being, enhances personal effectiveness, and cultivates resilience in the face of adversity. Through continued practice and self-reflection, empower yourself to challenge unhelpful thoughts, foster adaptive beliefs, and embrace opportunities for growth and fulfillment.

...

<u>Chapter 10: Building a Healthier Thought Pattern</u>

Building a healthier thought pattern involves cultivating cognitive habits and beliefs that promote emotional well-being, resilience, and positive life outcomes. In this chapter, we explore strategies, exercises, and principles for constructing and reinforcing healthier thought patterns through cognitive restructuring, mindfulness, self-compassion, and adaptive thinking skills.

Understanding Thought Patterns

Thought patterns are recurring cognitive processes that shape interpretations, emotional responses, and behavioral tendencies in response to internal and external stimuli. Healthy thought patterns involve balanced, constructive interpretations of experiences, self-affirming beliefs, and adaptive coping strategies. Key components of healthy thought patterns include:

1. **Positive Interpretations:** Foster positive interpretations of situations by focusing on strengths, opportunities, and constructive outcomes. Reframe challenges as opportunities for growth, learning, and personal development.

2. **Flexible Thinking:** Cultivate cognitive flexibility by considering multiple perspectives, alternative explanations, and creative solutions to problems. Adapt to changing circumstances with resilience and adaptability.

3. **Self-Compassion:** Practice self-compassion by treating oneself with kindness, understanding, and acceptance during difficult times or setbacks. Validate emotions, acknowledge vulnerabilities, and offer supportive self-talk.

Strategies for Building a Healthier Thought Pattern

Implement the following strategies to build and reinforce healthier thought patterns in daily life:

1. **Identify and Challenge Negative Thoughts:**

 - **Thought Monitoring:** Monitor automatic thoughts and cognitive patterns using thought records or journaling. Identify recurring themes, triggers, and emotional reactions associated with negative thoughts.

 - **Cognitive Restructuring:** Challenge cognitive distortions, such as all-or-nothing thinking, catastrophizing, and overgeneralization. Replace irrational thoughts with balanced, evidence-based alternatives supported by objective reality.

2. **Promote Positive Self-Talk and Affirmations:**

 - **Affirmative Statements:** Develop positive affirmations that reinforce self-worth, resilience, and personal strengths. Repeat affirmations regularly to internalize positive beliefs and counteract self-doubt or negative self-talk.

 - **Gratitude Practice:** Cultivate gratitude by acknowledging and appreciating positive aspects of life, relationships, and personal achievements. Maintain a gratitude journal to reflect on daily blessings and foster a positive mindset.

3. **Practice Mindfulness and Present-Moment Awareness:**

 - **Mindful Observation:** Engage in mindfulness practices, such as mindful breathing or body scan meditation, to cultivate present-moment awareness and non-judgmental acceptance of thoughts and emotions.

- **Mindful Reflection:** Reflect on thoughts, emotions, and sensory experiences with curiosity and openness. Notice cognitive patterns, emotional triggers, and opportunities for cognitive restructuring or self-regulation.

4. Develop Problem-Solving Skills and Adaptive Thinking:

- **Problem-Solving Strategies:** Use systematic problem-solving techniques, such as defining the problem, generating solutions, evaluating alternatives, and implementing action plans. Break down complex challenges into manageable steps.

- **Adaptive Thinking:** Adopt adaptive thinking styles, such as realistic optimism, constructive skepticism, and proactive planning. Anticipate challenges, develop contingency plans, and maintain flexibility in achieving goals.

5. Build Resilience and Coping Strategies:

- **Resilience-Building Activities:** Engage in activities that enhance resilience, such as physical exercise, relaxation techniques, and social support networks. Strengthen coping skills to manage stress, adversity, and life transitions effectively.

- **Cognitive Flexibility Training:** Practice cognitive flexibility exercises, such as brain teasers, puzzles, or creative problem-solving tasks. Challenge cognitive rigidity and enhance mental agility in adapting to new information or perspectives.

Techniques for Enhancing Thought Patterns

Explore effective techniques for enhancing thought patterns and promoting psychological well-being:

1. **Visualization and Imagery:**

- **Positive Visualization:** Use guided imagery or visualization techniques to imagine successful outcomes, positive experiences, or future goals. Visualize detailed scenarios and sensory details to reinforce optimism and motivation.

- **Imaginary Rehearsal:** Mentally rehearse challenging situations or performances to build confidence, reduce anxiety, and enhance performance readiness. Visualize adaptive responses and effective problem-solving strategies.

2. **Stress Management and Relaxation:**

- **Progressive Muscle Relaxation:** Practice progressive muscle relaxation to release tension, reduce physical stress symptoms, and promote relaxation. Sequentially tense and relax muscle groups to enhance body awareness and relaxation response.

- **Deep Breathing Exercises:** Use diaphragmatic breathing or deep breathing exercises to activate the body's relaxation response, reduce physiological arousal, and restore emotional equilibrium during stressful situations.

3. **Behavioral Activation and Goal Setting:**

- **Behavioral Activation:** Engage in pleasurable or meaningful activities that promote positive emotions, social engagement, and personal fulfillment. Schedule enjoyable activities to enhance mood, motivation, and overall well-being.

- **SMART Goals:** Set SMART (Specific, Measurable, Achievable, Relevant, Time-bound) goals to clarify objectives, prioritize tasks, and track progress toward personal or professional aspirations. Break goals into actionable steps for incremental achievement.

4. Cognitive Enhancement and Brain Health:

- **Lifelong Learning:** Embrace lifelong learning and intellectual curiosity to stimulate cognitive function, expand knowledge, and promote mental acuity. Pursue interests, hobbies, or educational pursuits that challenge and inspire personal growth.

- **Brain-Healthy Lifestyle:** Adopt a brain-healthy lifestyle that includes regular physical exercise, balanced nutrition, adequate sleep, and social engagement. Prioritize activities that support cognitive health and reduce cognitive decline.

Integrating Healthy Thought Patterns into Daily Routine

Integrate healthy thought patterns into daily routines to promote sustained emotional well-being and personal growth:

1. **Daily Reflection and Self-Assessment:**

- **Reflective Journaling:** Maintain a reflective journal to document thoughts, emotions, and insights gained from cognitive restructuring exercises. Track progress, identify patterns, and celebrate achievements in building healthier thought patterns.

- **Self-Assessment:** Evaluate personal strengths, areas for improvement, and growth opportunities based on cognitive restructuring outcomes. Identify strategies that enhance resilience, adaptive thinking, and emotional regulation.

2. **Mindful Self-Care Practices:**

- **Self-Care Rituals:** Establish mindful self-care rituals, such as morning meditation, evening relaxation routines, or nature walks, to nurture emotional well-being and reduce stress. Prioritize self-care activities that align with personal values and preferences.

- **Self-Compassion:** Practice self-compassion by offering kindness and understanding to oneself during challenging times or setbacks. Cultivate self-acceptance, forgive imperfections, and embrace opportunities for growth and learning.

3. **Social Support and Connection:**

- **Supportive Relationships:** Cultivate supportive relationships with friends, family members, or mentors who offer encouragement, empathy, and constructive feedback. Seek social support during times of stress or uncertainty to enhance resilience and emotional well-being.

- **Community Engagement:** Participate in community activities, volunteer opportunities, or group settings that promote social connection, belonging, and shared interests. Contribute to collective well-being and foster meaningful relationships.

Overcoming Challenges and Maintaining Progress

Navigate challenges in building healthier thought patterns with resilience, perseverance, and self-awareness:

1. **Persistence and Patience:**

- **Persistent Effort:** Maintain consistency in practicing cognitive restructuring techniques, mindfulness exercises, and self-care strategies. Embrace setbacks as opportunities for learning and refinement of coping skills.

- **Patience with Progress:** Recognize that building healthier thought patterns is a gradual process that requires patience and self-compassion. Celebrate small victories, acknowledge growth, and maintain optimism in achieving long-term goals.

2. Seeking Professional Guidance:

- **Therapeutic Support:** Consider seeking professional guidance from a therapist, counselor, or mental health professional trained in cognitive-behavioral therapy (CBT) or mindfulness-based interventions. Receive personalized support and evidence-based strategies for addressing persistent challenges.

- **Peer Support Networks:** Join peer support networks, online communities, or support groups focused on cognitive restructuring, mindfulness, or mental health resilience. Share experiences, exchange insights, and receive encouragement from individuals with similar goals.

Cultivating Lasting Change and Well-Being

Building a healthier thought pattern fosters lasting change, emotional resilience, and holistic well-being:

1. **Personal Growth:** Embrace opportunities for personal growth, self-discovery, and continuous learning through cognitive restructuring and mindfulness practices. Expand self-awareness, challenge limiting beliefs, and cultivate adaptive responses to life's challenges.

2. **Empowered Decision-Making:** Enhance decision-making skills by integrating healthy thought patterns, critical thinking, and emotional

intelligence. Evaluate options, anticipate consequences, and make informed choices that align with personal values and long-term goals.

3. **Quality of Life:** Improve overall quality of life by prioritizing mental health, emotional well-being, and self-care practices. Foster meaningful connections, pursue meaningful goals, and embrace a balanced lifestyle that supports physical, emotional, and cognitive vitality.

Conclusion: Embracing Healthier Thought Patterns

In conclusion, building a healthier thought pattern involves cultivating cognitive habits, beliefs, and strategies that promote emotional resilience, adaptive thinking, and personal growth. By implementing cognitive restructuring techniques, practicing mindfulness, nurturing self-compassion, and fostering adaptive behaviors, individuals empower themselves to navigate life's challenges with clarity, optimism, and resilience.

As you embark on the journey of building healthier thought patterns, reflect on your current cognitive habits, emotional responses, and beliefs about yourself and the world. Embrace the transformative power of cognitive restructuring, mindfulness practices, and self-compassionate self-talk in fostering emotional well-being and achieving personal fulfillment. Through ongoing self-reflection, practice, and integration of effective strategies, empower yourself to build resilience, cultivate positive thought patterns, and embrace a fulfilling life grounded in self-awareness and emotional balance.

...

Chapter 11: Overcoming Self-Doubt and Negative Self-Talk

Self-doubt and negative self-talk are common psychological challenges that can undermine confidence, hinder personal growth, and impact overall well-being. In this chapter, we explore strategies, exercises, and principles for overcoming self-doubt, challenging negative self-talk, and cultivating self-confidence and resilience.

Understanding Self-Doubt and Negative Self-Talk

Self-doubt refers to the lack of confidence in one's abilities, decisions, or self-worth. Negative self-talk involves critical or pessimistic internal dialogue that reinforces self-doubt, perpetuates limiting beliefs, and contributes to emotional distress. Key characteristics of self-doubt and negative self-talk include:

1. **Internal Criticism:** Engaging in self-criticism, self-blame, or harsh judgments regarding personal performance, appearance, or perceived shortcomings.

2. **Perfectionism:** Setting unrealistically high standards, fearing failure or mistakes, and experiencing anxiety or frustration when expectations are not met.

3. **Comparison:** Comparing oneself unfavorably to others, experiencing envy or insecurity, and attributing success or failure to personal deficiencies.

Strategies for Overcoming Self-Doubt

Implement the following strategies to overcome self-doubt and foster self-confidence:

1. **Recognize and Challenge Negative Thoughts:**

- **Mindful Awareness:** Practice mindfulness to observe and identify negative thoughts, emotions, and self-critical tendencies without judgment. Notice triggers, cognitive patterns, and emotional reactions associated with self-doubt.

- **Cognitive Restructuring:** Challenge negative self-talk by questioning the validity and accuracy of self-critical thoughts. Replace irrational beliefs with balanced, evidence-based alternatives that promote self-compassion and realistic self-appraisal.

2. **Promote Self-Compassion and Acceptance:**

- **Self-Compassionate Mindset:** Cultivate self-compassion by treating oneself with kindness, understanding, and acceptance during moments of self-doubt or difficulty. Offer supportive self-talk, acknowledge personal challenges, and validate emotions without self-judgment.

- **Radical Acceptance:** Practice radical acceptance by embracing imperfections, setbacks, and uncertainties as part of the human experience. Let go of unrealistic expectations, self-criticism, and the need for constant approval or validation.

3. **Challenge Perfectionism and Unrealistic Standards:**

- **Setting Realistic Goals:** Establish achievable goals that align with personal values, strengths, and priorities. Break down larger tasks into manageable steps, celebrate progress, and acknowledge effort regardless of outcomes.

- **Embrace Growth Mindset**: Adopt a growth mindset by viewing challenges, setbacks, and mistakes as opportunities for learning, improvement, and personal development. Emphasize effort, persistence, and resilience in achieving long-term goals.

Techniques for Challenging Negative Self-Talk

Explore effective techniques for challenging and reframing negative self-talk:

1. **Thought Stopping:**

  - **Cue Interruption:** Interrupt negative self-talk by using a physical or verbal cue, such as saying "Stop!" or visualizing a stop sign. Disrupt repetitive thought patterns and redirect attention to positive affirmations or constructive thoughts.

  - **Replacing Thoughts:** Replace negative statements with affirming, compassionate, and realistic self-statements. Use phrases like "I am capable and resilient," "I deserve kindness and understanding," or "I am learning and growing from challenges."

2. **Cognitive Distancing:**

  - **Thought Defusion:** Practice thought defusion techniques to create psychological distance from negative self-talk. View thoughts as passing mental events rather than accurate reflections of reality. Label self-critical thoughts as "just thoughts" rather than facts.

  - **Metaphorical Reframing:** Reinterpret negative self-talk using humor, exaggeration, or playful imagery. Transform harsh self-criticisms into lighthearted or compassionate perspectives that reduce emotional intensity and promote self-acceptance.

3. **Creating a Positive Self-Concept:**

- **Self-Affirmations:** Develop positive affirmations that reinforce self-worth, competence, and personal strengths. Repeat affirmations regularly to internalize positive beliefs and counteract self-doubt or negative comparisons.

- **Strengths Identification:** Identify and celebrate personal strengths, accomplishments, and qualities that contribute to self-confidence and resilience. Recognize past successes, perseverance in overcoming challenges, and growth from adversity.

Building Self-Confidence and Resilience

Enhance self-confidence and resilience through intentional practices and mindset shifts:

1. **Skills Development:**

- **Skill-Building Activities:** Engage in activities that promote skill development, competence, and mastery in areas of interest or professional growth. Seek opportunities for learning, practice, and feedback to enhance self-efficacy and confidence.

- **Competence Reinforcement:** Reinforce feelings of competence by setting achievable goals, acquiring new knowledge or skills, and recognizing progress and improvement over time.

2. **Positive Visualization and Imagery:**

- **Visualization Exercises:** Use guided imagery or visualization techniques to imagine successful outcomes, positive interactions, or future achievements. Visualize detailed scenarios and sensory details to enhance confidence and motivation.

- **Imaginary Rehearsal:** Mentally rehearse challenging situations or goals to build confidence, reduce anxiety, and prepare for effective performance or decision-making.

3. **Seeking Support and Feedback:**

- **Social Support Networks:** Seek support from trusted friends, family members, or mentors who offer encouragement, empathy, and constructive feedback. Share experiences, discuss challenges, and receive perspective on self-doubt and personal growth.

- **Professional Guidance:** Consider consulting with a therapist, counselor, or coach specializing in self-esteem, confidence-building, or cognitive-behavioral techniques. Receive personalized support, strategies, and accountability in overcoming self-doubt.

Embracing Growth and Personal Empowerment

Embrace growth and personal empowerment by cultivating self-compassion, challenging negative self-talk, and fostering resilience:

1. **Emotional Resilience:** Develop emotional resilience by practicing self-awareness, mindfulness, and adaptive coping strategies. Respond to setbacks, criticism, or uncertainty with clarity, composure, and proactive problem-solving.

2. **Authentic Self-Expression:**

- **Authenticity:** Embrace authenticity by honoring personal values, beliefs, and aspirations in decision-making, relationships, and life pursuits. Align actions with intrinsic motivations, genuine interests, and meaningful goals.

- **Self-Validation:** Validate personal experiences, emotions, and achievements without seeking external validation or approval. Trust in personal strengths, resilience, and capacity for growth in navigating life's challenges.

3. **Celebrating Progress and Achievements:**

- **Milestone Recognition:** Celebrate milestones, achievements, and personal growth experiences along the journey of overcoming self-doubt. Acknowledge progress, resilience, and perseverance in pursuing goals and aspirations.

Conclusion: Cultivating Self-Confidence and Emotional Resilience

In conclusion, overcoming self-doubt and negative self-talk involves cultivating self-awareness, challenging irrational beliefs, and fostering self-compassion and resilience. By practicing cognitive restructuring techniques, mindfulness, and positive self-talk, individuals empower themselves to build self-confidence, embrace personal growth, and navigate life's challenges with resilience and authenticity.

As you explore strategies for overcoming self-doubt in your own life, reflect on your unique strengths, values, and aspirations. Embrace the transformative power of self-compassion, positive self-talk, and growth mindset in fostering emotional well-being and achieving personal fulfillment. Through ongoing practice, self-reflection, and supportive relationships, empower yourself to overcome self-doubt, cultivate resilience, and embrace a fulfilling life grounded in confidence, authenticity, and empowered self-expression.

...

<u>Chapter 12: Developing Emotional Resilience</u>

Emotional resilience is the ability to adapt and bounce back from adversity, trauma, stress, or significant life challenges. It involves coping effectively with difficulties, maintaining emotional stability, and navigating setbacks with optimism and determination. In this chapter, we explore strategies, practices, and principles for developing and strengthening emotional resilience.

Understanding Emotional Resilience

Emotional resilience encompasses psychological processes and coping mechanisms that promote adaptive responses to adversity. Key aspects of emotional resilience include:

1. **Adaptive Coping Strategies:** Engaging in proactive behaviors, problem-solving skills, and emotional regulation techniques to manage stress, uncertainty, and setbacks effectively.

2. **Positive Mindset:** Maintaining optimism, perseverance, and a growth mindset in facing challenges, setbacks, or unexpected changes in circumstances.

3. **Supportive Relationships:** Seeking social support, nurturing meaningful connections, and receiving empathy, encouragement, and practical assistance during difficult times.

Strategies for Developing Emotional Resilience

Implement the following strategies to cultivate and strengthen emotional resilience in everyday life:

1. **Build Self-Awareness and Emotional Regulation:**

- **Mindfulness Practices:** Practice mindfulness meditation, deep breathing exercises, or body scan techniques to cultivate present-moment awareness, reduce stress, and enhance emotional regulation.

- **Emotion Identification:** Identify and label emotions accurately to understand their underlying causes, triggers, and effects on thoughts, behaviors, and physical sensations.

2. **Cognitive Restructuring and Adaptive Thinking:**

- **Challenge Cognitive Distortions:** Recognize and challenge irrational beliefs, negative self-talk, and cognitive distortions that contribute to pessimism, self-doubt, or emotional distress.

- **Reframe Challenges:** Reframe setbacks or obstacles as opportunities for learning, growth, and personal development. Adopt a growth mindset that emphasizes resilience, effort, and adaptive responses to adversity.

3. **Develop Problem-Solving Skills:**

- **Systematic Problem-Solving:** Use systematic problem-solving techniques, such as defining the problem, generating solutions, evaluating alternatives, and implementing action plans.

- **Decision-Making:** Make informed decisions based on thorough analysis, consideration of consequences, and alignment with personal values, goals, and priorities.

4. **Cultivate Social Support Networks:**

- **Seek Support:** Reach out to trusted friends, family members, or mentors for emotional support, practical assistance, and constructive feedback during challenging times.

- **Join Communities:** Participate in community activities, support groups, or online forums to connect with others who share similar experiences, interests, or goals.

5. Practice Adaptability and Flexibility:

- **Adapt to Change:** Embrace uncertainty, navigate unexpected changes, and adjust plans or expectations based on evolving circumstances.

- **Flexibility:** Maintain flexibility in thinking, problem-solving, and decision-making to respond effectively to new challenges, opportunities, or setbacks.

Techniques for Enhancing Emotional Resilience

Explore effective techniques for enhancing emotional resilience and promoting psychological well-being:

1. Stress Management and Relaxation Techniques:

- **Progressive Muscle Relaxation:** Practice progressive muscle relaxation to release tension, reduce physical stress symptoms, and promote relaxation.

- **Deep Breathing Exercises:** Use diaphragmatic breathing or deep breathing exercises to activate the body's relaxation response, reduce physiological arousal, and restore emotional equilibrium.

2. Cognitive Flexibility and Adaptation:

- **Exposure Therapy:** Gradually expose oneself to feared or anxiety-provoking situations to build tolerance, resilience, and adaptive coping skills.

- **Problem-Solving Practice:** Engage in problem-solving activities, puzzles, or creative tasks to stimulate cognitive flexibility, enhance problem-solving skills, and promote adaptive thinking.

3. **Positive Psychology Interventions:**

- **Gratitude Practices:** Cultivate gratitude by keeping a gratitude journal, expressing appreciation to others, or reflecting on daily blessings and meaningful experiences.

- **Strengths Identification:** Identify and leverage personal strengths, talents, and resources to overcome challenges, achieve goals, and enhance overall well-being.

4. **Resilience-Building Activities:**

- **Physical Exercise:** Engage in regular physical activity, such as aerobic exercise, strength training, or yoga, to reduce stress, improve mood, and enhance resilience.

- **Creative Expression:** Express emotions, thoughts, or experiences through creative outlets, such as writing, art, music, or dance, to promote self-expression and emotional healing.

Integrating Emotional Resilience into Daily Life

Integrate emotional resilience practices into daily routines to foster sustained well-being and adaptive coping:

1. **Self-Care Rituals and Well-Being Practices:**

- **Self-Care:** Prioritize self-care activities that nurture physical, emotional, and mental well-being, such as adequate sleep, nutritious diet, hydration, and relaxation techniques.

- **Mindful Awareness:** Cultivate mindful awareness of thoughts, emotions, and sensory experiences to enhance self-awareness, reduce stress, and promote emotional regulation.

2. **Continuous Learning and Personal Growth:**

- **Lifelong Learning:** Pursue ongoing learning opportunities, hobbies, or interests that stimulate curiosity, expand knowledge, and promote personal growth.

- **Adaptive Skills Development:** Develop adaptive skills, such as resilience, emotional intelligence, and effective communication, to navigate interpersonal relationships and professional challenges.

3. **Reflective Practice and Goal Setting:**

- **Reflection:** Engage in reflective practices, journaling, or self-assessment to evaluate personal strengths, growth areas, and progress in developing emotional resilience.

- **Goal Setting:** Set SMART (Specific, Measurable, Achievable, Relevant, Time-bound) goals to clarify objectives, prioritize tasks, and track progress toward enhancing emotional resilience and achieving personal aspirations.

Overcoming Challenges and Building Resilience

Navigate challenges in developing emotional resilience with persistence, self-compassion, and adaptive coping strategies:

1. **Persistence and Adaptability:**

- **Perseverance:** Maintain motivation and commitment to enhancing emotional resilience despite setbacks, obstacles, or temporary setbacks.

- **Adaptability:** Adjust strategies, seek support, and learn from experiences to build adaptive coping skills and effectively manage stress, adversity, or unexpected challenges.

2. **Seeking Support and Professional Guidance:**

- **Social Support Networks:** Connect with supportive relationships, peer groups, or community resources to receive encouragement, empathy, and practical assistance during difficult times.

- **Therapeutic Support:** Consider consulting with a therapist, counselor, or mental health professional for personalized guidance, cognitive-behavioral techniques, and resilience-building interventions.

Cultivating Lasting Emotional Resilience and Well-Being

Developing emotional resilience promotes lasting well-being, adaptive coping skills, and psychological strength in navigating life's challenges:

1. **Adaptive Coping Strategies:** Implement adaptive coping strategies, problem-solving skills, and emotion regulation techniques to manage stress, uncertainty, and adversity effectively.

2. **Self-Compassion and Reflection:** Practice self-compassion, self-awareness, and reflective practices to enhance emotional resilience, foster personal growth, and cultivate a positive mindset.

3. **Community Engagement and Contribution:** Participate in community activities, volunteer opportunities, or social initiatives that promote social connection, belonging, and collective well-being.

Conclusion: Embracing Emotional Resilience

In conclusion, developing emotional resilience involves cultivating adaptive coping strategies, fostering self-awareness, and embracing challenges as opportunities for growth and personal development. By practicing mindfulness, cognitive flexibility, and proactive problem-solving, individuals empower themselves to navigate adversity, strengthen resilience, and foster well-being in various aspects of life.

As you explore strategies for developing emotional resilience in your own life, reflect on your unique strengths, values, and aspirations. Embrace the transformative power of resilience-building practices, supportive relationships, and self-compassionate self-talk in enhancing psychological well-being and achieving personal fulfillment. Through ongoing practice, self-reflection, and integration of effective strategies, empower yourself to build emotional resilience, navigate life's challenges with confidence, and embrace a fulfilling life grounded in adaptive coping and emotional strength.

...

<u>Chapter 13: The Journey to Mental Clarity</u>

Achieving mental clarity involves cultivating a state of clear thinking, focus, and emotional balance amidst the complexities of daily life. In this chapter, we explore strategies, practices, and principles for enhancing mental clarity, reducing cognitive overwhelm, and fostering psychological well-being.

Understanding Mental Clarity

Mental clarity encompasses the ability to think clearly, make decisions effectively, and maintain focus on tasks or goals without undue distraction or cognitive overload. Key components of mental clarity include:

1. **Clear Thinking:** Enhancing cognitive processes, logical reasoning, and problem-solving skills to navigate complex information and make informed decisions.

2. **Emotional Balance:** Managing emotions, reducing stress, and promoting psychological well-being to maintain clarity of thought and perspective.

3. **Focus and Concentration:** Improving attention span, concentration, and mindfulness to sustain productivity, creativity, and mental resilience.

Strategies for Enhancing Mental Clarity

Implement the following strategies to cultivate and enhance mental clarity in daily life:

1. **Mindfulness Practices:**

- **Mindful Awareness:** Practice mindfulness meditation, deep breathing exercises, or mindful walking to cultivate present-moment awareness, reduce mental clutter, and enhance focus.

- **Mindful Eating:** Engage in mindful eating practices to savor flavors, textures, and sensations, promoting conscious decision-making and reducing distractions during meals.

2. **Organizational Strategies:**

- **Prioritization:** Use task prioritization techniques, such as Eisenhower's Urgent/Important matrix or ABC prioritization, to manage time effectively and focus attention on high-priority tasks.

- **Decluttering:** Organize physical and digital environments to reduce visual and mental clutter, enhance productivity, and create a conducive space for clear thinking.

3. **Cognitive Enhancement Techniques**:

- **Brain Exercises:** Engage in brain-stimulating activities, such as puzzles, crosswords, or memory games, to improve cognitive function, mental agility, and problem-solving abilities.

- **Lifelong Learning:** Pursue continuous learning opportunities, hobbies, or intellectual pursuits that stimulate curiosity, expand knowledge, and promote cognitive clarity.

4. **Stress Management and Relaxation:**

- **Stress Reduction:** Practice stress management techniques, such as progressive muscle relaxation, deep breathing exercises, or yoga, to alleviate tension, promote relaxation, and restore mental clarity.

- **Digital Detox:** Limit screen time, digital distractions, and information overload by scheduling technology breaks or implementing digital detox practices to recharge mental energy.

Techniques for Cultivating Mental Clarity

Explore effective techniques for cultivating mental clarity and promoting cognitive well-being:

1. **Visualization and Imagery:**

- **Positive Visualization:** Use guided imagery or visualization techniques to imagine successful outcomes, visualize goals, or mentally rehearse challenging situations to enhance clarity and confidence.

- **Imaginary Scenarios:** Create mental scenarios or simulations to anticipate challenges, explore solutions, and prepare for decision-making or problem-solving in various contexts.

2. **Journaling and Reflection:**

- **Reflective Writing:** Maintain a journal or reflective writing practice to clarify thoughts, process emotions, and gain insights into personal experiences, goals, or challenges.

- **Gratitude Journaling:** Cultivate gratitude by recording daily blessings, positive experiences, or moments of appreciation to foster a positive mindset and enhance mental clarity.

3. **Time Management and Productivity:**
- **Time Blocking:** Allocate dedicated time blocks for specific tasks, projects, or activities to minimize multitasking, reduce cognitive load, and optimize focus and productivity.

- **Pomodoro Technique:** Use the Pomodoro Technique or similar time-management methods to work in focused intervals (e.g., 25 minutes of work followed by 5 minutes of rest) to maintain mental clarity and sustain productivity.

4. Healthy Lifestyle Habits:

- **Sleep Hygiene:** Prioritize adequate sleep and establish consistent sleep routines to promote cognitive function, memory consolidation, and mental clarity.

- **Nutrition and Hydration:** Maintain a balanced diet, stay hydrated, and consume brain-boosting nutrients (e.g., omega-3 fatty acids, antioxidants) to support cognitive health and mental clarity.

Integrating Mental Clarity into Daily Routine

Integrate mental clarity practices into daily routines to foster sustained well-being and cognitive performance:

1. Morning Rituals and Mindful Start:

- **Morning Routine:** Establish a morning ritual that includes mindfulness practices, goal setting, or reflective journaling to cultivate mental clarity and set positive intentions for the day ahead.

- **Mindful Beginnings:** Start each day with mindful breathing, grounding exercises, or gratitude practice to center attention, reduce mental chatter, and enhance focus on priorities.

2. Workplace Strategies and Environment:

- **Workspace Optimization:** Create an ergonomic, organized workspace with minimal distractions, adequate lighting, and ergonomic furniture to promote focus, creativity, and mental clarity.

- **Digital Boundaries:** Set boundaries for email notifications, social media use, and digital communication to minimize interruptions, maintain concentration, and preserve mental energy.

3. **Mindful Communication and Relationships:**

- **Active Listening:** Practice active listening techniques, empathetic communication, and non-verbal cues to enhance understanding, clarity, and meaningful connections in interpersonal relationships.

- **Conflict Resolution:** Approach conflicts or disagreements with openness, empathy, and constructive communication strategies to foster clarity, mutual respect, and resolution.

Overcoming Mental Barriers and Maintaining Clarity

Navigate mental barriers to clarity with resilience, self-awareness, and adaptive coping strategies:

1. **Self-Reflection and Adjustment:**

- **Self-Assessment**: Evaluate personal strengths, growth areas, and emotional triggers that impact mental clarity. Adjust strategies, seek support, and learn from experiences to enhance cognitive resilience and well-being.

- **Adaptive Strategies:** Experiment with different techniques, adjust routines, and incorporate feedback to optimize cognitive performance, manage stress, and maintain clarity in challenging situations.

2. Seeking Professional Guidance and Support:

- **Therapeutic Support:** Consider consulting with a therapist, counselor, or mental health professional for personalized guidance, cognitive-behavioral strategies, or stress management techniques to enhance mental clarity and emotional well-being.

- **Peer Support Networks:** Connect with supportive communities, peer groups, or online forums focused on mindfulness, cognitive enhancement, or personal development to share insights, resources, and encouragement.

Cultivating Lasting Mental Clarity and Cognitive Well-Being

Cultivating mental clarity promotes cognitive well-being, enhances decision-making, and fosters personal growth and fulfillment:

1. **Cognitive Wellness:** Embrace lifelong learning, cognitive challenges, and personal growth opportunities to stimulate mental clarity, creativity, and adaptive thinking skills.

2. **Self-Mastery and Resilience:** Develop self-mastery, emotional resilience, and adaptive coping strategies to navigate uncertainty, overcome challenges, and sustain mental clarity in various aspects of life.

3. **Holistic Well-Being:** Prioritize holistic well-being by integrating mental clarity practices, self-care rituals, and healthy lifestyle habits that support cognitive function, emotional balance, and overall quality of life.

Conclusion: Embracing Mental Clarity

In conclusion, the journey to mental clarity involves cultivating mindfulness, enhancing cognitive resilience, and fostering emotional balance to navigate challenges, make informed decisions, and sustain well-being. By integrating mindfulness practices, organizational strategies, and cognitive enhancement techniques into daily routines, individuals empower themselves to achieve clarity of thought, focus, and purpose in pursuing personal and professional aspirations.

As you explore strategies for enhancing mental clarity in your own life, reflect on your unique strengths, values, and aspirations. Embrace the transformative power of mindfulness, cognitive flexibility, and self-reflection in promoting cognitive wellness and achieving a fulfilling life grounded in clarity, resilience, and empowered decision-making. Through ongoing practice, self-awareness, and integration of effective strategies, empower yourself to cultivate mental clarity, navigate life's complexities with confidence, and embrace a purpose-driven journey of personal growth and well-being.

...

Conclusion: Embracing a Balanced Mindset

Achieving a balanced mindset involves cultivating emotional resilience, fostering mental clarity, and embracing adaptive thinking to navigate life's challenges with clarity, purpose, and well-being. In this concluding chapter, we reflect on the importance of balance in mental health, strategies for promoting emotional equilibrium, and integrating mindfulness into daily life for sustained well-being.

The Importance of Emotional Resilience and Mental Clarity

Emotional resilience and mental clarity are foundational to navigating the complexities of modern life. They enable individuals to manage stress, adapt to change, and maintain psychological well-being amidst adversity and uncertainty. By developing emotional resilience, individuals build the capacity to bounce back from setbacks, regulate emotions effectively, and cultivate a positive mindset that promotes resilience in the face of challenges.

Mental clarity enhances cognitive function, improves decision-making, and fosters creativity and innovation. It involves the ability to think critically, solve problems efficiently, and maintain focus amidst distractions. By fostering mental clarity, individuals optimize cognitive performance, reduce cognitive overload, and enhance productivity and efficiency in various aspects of life.

Strategies for Promoting Emotional Equilibrium

Implementing strategies to promote emotional equilibrium enhances overall well-being and supports mental health:

1. **Mindfulness Practices:**

- **Mindful Awareness:** Cultivate present-moment awareness through mindfulness meditation, deep breathing exercises, or mindful movement practices. Mindfulness reduces stress, enhances emotional regulation, and promotes clarity of thought.

- **Mindful Living**: Integrate mindfulness into daily routines by practicing mindful eating, mindful communication, and mindful engagement with tasks or activities. Mindful living fosters self-awareness, enhances concentration, and promotes emotional resilience.

2. Emotional Regulation Techniques:

- **Emotion Recognition:** Identify and label emotions accurately to understand their impact on thoughts, behaviors, and well-being. Emotional awareness promotes self-regulation and adaptive responses to emotional experiences.

- **Cognitive Restructuring:** Challenge negative thought patterns, replace irrational beliefs with balanced perspectives, and cultivate self-compassion and positive self-talk. Cognitive restructuring enhances resilience, reduces emotional distress, and promotes a balanced mindset.

3. Stress Management Strategies:

- **Stress Reduction:** Practice stress management techniques, such as progressive muscle relaxation, visualization, or time-management strategies, to alleviate tension, enhance resilience, and restore emotional equilibrium.

- **Healthy Coping Mechanisms:** Engage in activities that promote relaxation, creativity, or physical exercise to reduce stress, improve mood, and support emotional well-being.

Integrating Mindfulness into Daily Life

Integrating mindfulness practices into daily life promotes sustained well-being and enhances mental clarity:

1. **Morning Rituals and Mindful Beginnings:**

  - **Morning Routine:** Establish a morning ritual that includes mindfulness exercises, gratitude practice, or goal-setting to set a positive tone for the day ahead. Morning rituals enhance focus, clarity, and emotional resilience.

  - **Intention Setting:** Set intentions for the day, aligning actions with personal values, goals, and priorities. Intention setting fosters mindfulness, promotes proactive decision-making, and supports emotional balance throughout the day.

2. **Mindful Engagement with Challenges:**

  - **Adaptive Thinking:** Approach challenges with a growth mindset, viewing setbacks as opportunities for learning, growth, and personal development. Adaptive thinking enhances resilience, promotes problem-solving skills, and fosters a balanced perspective on adversity.

  - **Acceptance and Letting Go:** Practice radical acceptance of circumstances beyond personal control, letting go of perfectionism, and embracing imperfections and uncertainties with compassion and resilience.

Embracing a Purpose-Driven Life

Embracing a purpose-driven life involves aligning actions with meaningful goals, values, and aspirations:

1. **Clarifying Personal Values:** Identify core values that guide decision-making, behavior, and life choices. Clarifying personal values promotes authenticity, enhances self-awareness, and supports mental clarity and emotional well-being.

2. **Goal Setting and Achievement:**

- **SMART Goals:** Set specific, measurable, achievable, relevant, and time-bound (SMART) goals to clarify objectives, prioritize tasks, and track progress toward personal and professional aspirations.

- **Celebrating Milestones:** Acknowledge achievements, milestones, and personal growth experiences along the journey of pursuing goals. Celebrating successes reinforces motivation, boosts self-confidence, and promotes a positive mindset.

3. **Fostering Meaningful Connections:**

- **Nurturing Relationships:** Cultivate meaningful connections with supportive friends, family members, or community networks. Nurturing relationships promotes social support, enhances resilience, and fosters emotional well-being.

- **Contributing to Community:** Engage in volunteer work, community service, or social initiatives that align with personal values and contribute to collective well-being. Community involvement enhances fulfillment, promotes empathy, and supports mental health.

Conclusion: Embracing Balance and Well-Being

In conclusion, embracing a balanced mindset involves cultivating emotional resilience, fostering mental clarity, and integrating mindfulness into daily life to promote well-being and navigate challenges with clarity, purpose, and resilience. By practicing mindfulness, emotional regulation, and adaptive thinking, individuals empower themselves to manage stress effectively, enhance cognitive function, and sustain psychological well-being amidst life's complexities.

As you embark on your journey towards balance and well-being, reflect on your unique strengths, values, and aspirations. Embrace the transformative power of mindfulness practices, emotional resilience, and purpose-driven living in fostering a balanced mindset and achieving fulfillment in various aspects of life. Through ongoing practice, self-awareness, and integration of effective strategies, empower yourself to cultivate resilience, embrace a balanced perspective, and thrive in pursuing personal growth, meaningful connections, and a purpose-driven life grounded in clarity, resilience, and well-being.

...